YESTERDAY'S RADICALS

YESTERDAY'S RADICALS

*A Study of the Affinity between Unitarianism and Broad Church
Anglicanism in the Nineteenth Century*

BY

DENNIS G. WIGMORE-BEDDOES

FOREWORD
by
ALEC VIDLER

JAMES CLARKE & CO. LTD.
Cambridge and London

Published by James Clarke & Co. Ltd.
7 All Saints Passage, Cambridge, England

Printed in Great Britain by
Latimer Trend & Co. Ltd., Plymouth

Contents

"The Broad Church party ... if it was in kinship with any other Church besides the Church of England, was in kinship with Unitarianism."

Lyulph Stanley

"It cannot be denied that there is much closer theological sympathy between ourselves and the Broad Church party in the National Church than there is between us and any section of orthodox Nonconformists."

The Inquirer (editorial),
14th January 1865

Foreword

When the author of this book allowed me to read the thesis from which it has sprung, I became keenly interested in it. It seemed to me to break fresh ground in the study of nineteenth-century English divinity and to open up a number of questions that invited further investigation. I am therefore glad to hear that the book is to be published and I hope that many other readers will find the material which it contains as interesting as I did and that it will be a spur to further studies in the same and adjacent fields.

ALEC VIDLER

February 1970

7

Preface

Today we are living in a period in which the term "heresy" is losing currency in theological circles, and I hope that this may lead to a more sympathetic reading of the views set forth in this book than would have been possible in the theological atmosphere that prevailed in the period before the publication of Dr. John Robinson's *Honest to God*.

If there was an affinity between the Unitarians and Broad Churchmen of yesterday, it may also be said that they both have certain affinities with the radicals of today, though the latter have so far been more successful in avoiding the label "heretic". This is not to say that there are not subtle and significant differences between the approach and the temperament of the nineteenth-century liberals and the twentieth-century radicals. But a similarity exists, and I believe that a consideration of the radical position of today may be illuminated by placing it against the background discussed in this book.

One of the most heartening developments of today, of course, by comparison with yesterday, is the wider front upon which the current freedom of theological discussion is being developed. Yet even here the Anglican Church has continued to take the lead, at least in the British Isles. Unitarianism, regrettably, has failed to maintain the vanguard position it once held, though it has produced valuable pioneer work in certain fields; and it is to be hoped that in the current theological climate, in which doctrinal restrictions are coming to be more and more relaxed, it will be possible for it to exert itself again, with fresh creative and critical power, without having to work under the handicap of the label of "heresy". By the standards of yesterday no candid observer could deny that many of today's radicals are far more deserving of this label than either yesterday's Broad Churchmen or today's Unitarians.

I imagine that I am not the first person to find difficulty in writing a preface to a book which in substance was written several years ago. But the thesis that was presented for the degree of M.A. of Birmingham University stands so closely behind, and within, this book that I have decided to let part of its original preface, now called the Prologue, remain. The references to the title in the Prologue refer to what is now the sub-title.

Had I possessed the inclination I suppose that I could have written this book in a more popular style, but I have resisted this temptation, in the interests of providing the kind of documentation that is needed in this important, but neglected field of study; and I hope that my readers will refer to the sometimes copious notes, and use in this connection the help given in the table of contents towards finding them more easily.

It remains for me to thank Dr. Vidler for so kindly writing a Foreword, and my wife for the constant encouragement that she has given me in connection with the publication of this book and for compiling the index.

Not least must I thank the Hibbert Trust, the Daniel Jones Fund, the Ulster Unitarian Christian Association, and my own church, the First Presbyterian Church, Belfast, for generous grants towards publication.

This work, it should be added, secured the Earl Morse Wilbur Prize for Historical Research from the American Unitarian Historical Society.

D. G. WIGMORE-BEDDOES

February 1970

Prologue

The late Dr. Barnes, Bishop of Birmingham, was sometimes known as "the Unitarian Bishop"; and between the Anglican Modernist and the Unitarian of the present day there still exists a measure of theological sympathy. This was even more true of the Anglican Broad Churchmen and the Unitarians of a century ago; and probably most people familiar with the subject of the Broad Church or with Unitarianism in the nineteenth century are aware that an affinity existed between them. But the matter has never been the subject of investigation; and it is one thing to be vaguely aware that there was some affinity, and quite another to know just what that affinity was. In this work I have attempted to show, not only that there *was* an affinity, but also what its features were.

The illustrative material in the form of quotations—which are necessarily rather numerous, though they have been cut down to the minimum required to establish the points maintained—has generally been spread, it will be seen, over the whole century, so as to show, where this is the case, that the particular feature referred to was not an isolated phenomenon, but something true of the whole period under discussion. Indeed, it is even hoped that some of the passages cited, and some of the descriptions given, will suitably preserve, and conveniently summarize, a number of the more interesting features of Unitarian and Anglican Broad Church literature. All too often, this material, Unitarian literature in particular, is difficult to obtain and badly preserved.

Lest the latter remarks should be taken to indicate any particular theological bias, I should hasten to add that throughout this work I have endeavoured to be as fair and objective as possible, and it is a matter of some gratification to me that one of my first readers, my typist, was unable to decide whether I was an Anglican or a Unitarian! This, however—along with my avoidance of the terms "I" and "we" in the text, both of which I eschew on grounds of personal taste—must not be taken to indicate that in the following pages there will be found any lack of decision where decision is due; and I suspect that both in the selection and arrangement of the material, quite apart from my conclusions, there will be found a personal interpretation which everyone will not share.

A word must be added about the title, which, in spite of the absence of the term in the text, refers to Broad Church *Anglicanism*. This is quite deliberate, as by this term, I wish to avoid any suspicion, which the frequent use of the term "Anglican Broad Church" might be taken to indicate, of a tendency to think of the Broad Church as a separate entity entirely divorced from the rest of Anglicanism; but the constant use, in close juxtaposition, of two words—Unitarianism and Anglicanism—both ending in "ism" is not particularly attractive, and so, in the text, the popular term of the latter half of the nineteenth century, viz., "Broad Church", has been employed. And though the term "Anglicanism" was not used before, nor "Broad Church", in respect of an actual living party, very much after, the nineteenth century, I have not felt pedantic enough to avoid the use of the phrase "in the nineteenth century" in the title.

And now the time has come for me to undertake the pleasant duty of expressing my thanks, which in the first place must be accorded to the University of Birmingham for granting me in 1958 the Francis Corder Clayton Scholarship, which enabled me to begin this research; and in this connection, as also for his very kind and helpful encouragement during the first year of my work, I should particularly like to mention the Rev. Professor G. W. H. Lampe, M.A., D.D., now of Cambridge. To the Rev. J. C. Dickinson, M.A., B.Litt., F.S.A., who succeeded him as my supervisor, thanks are also due for helpful criticism, and suggestions regarding general presentation. Not least I must express my thanks to the Rev. H. L. Short, M.A., Warden of Manchester College, Oxford, who not only suggested the field for my enquiries, but who has also given very kind help when doubt has occasionally arisen with regard to certain points of Unitarian history. To the Principal of Manchester College, Oxford, the Rev. L. A. Garrard, B.D., M.A., LL.D., my thanks are also due for having provided facilities for research at Oxford. Nor must I fail to mention the valued assistance of the Rev. A. E. Peaston, M.A., B.Litt., F.R.Hist.S., who very kindly provided me with an unpublished list of Unitarian liturgies, some use of which I have made in Chapter 4. To all these good people; to the several correspondents, who have answered a number of enquiries; to the staffs of numerous libraries, not least that of the Reference Library, Birmingham; and to my parents who have endured much inconvenience at home as the work has gone ahead I express my grateful thanks.

It was with an Anglican Dr. Barnes that I began this preface, and it is with the words of a Unitarian Dr. Barnes (1747–1810), the first Divinity tutor at Manchester College, that I will end, when I say of this work, as he did in respect of Manchester College, where several of the leading figures mentioned in the following pages carried out their most conspicuous work: I dedicate it "to Truth, to Liberty, to Religion".

D. G. WIGMORE-BEDDOES

September 1963

CHAPTER I

Historical Introduction

Today the term "Broad Church" is not a very familiar one. But in the nineteenth century this was not the case. The Broad Churchmen were a significant body of men who could not be ignored, and the term "Broad Church" stood, as the *Oxford Dictionary of the Christian Church* rightly defines it, as a term to designate "those in the C. of E. who objected to positive definition in theology and sought to interpret the Anglican formularies in a broad and liberal sense".[1] The Broad Churchmen constituted the progressive wing of the Anglican Church. They were interested in science, in Biblical criticism, in a rational approach to religion, and were leaders in the attempt to relate the Church's teaching to the new thought and conditions of the nineteenth century. As such they were the Latitudinarians and Modernists of their age.

But the Broad Churchmen were not alone in their task of criticizing tradition in the light of modern knowledge and enlarging experience with a view to reformulation in service of modern needs: the nineteenth-century Unitarians, who under the guidance of such leaders as James Martineau and John James Tayler, came to regard reason and conscience as the criteria of belief and practice, were possessed of a similar spirit. And it is the purpose of this book to examine the affinity which existed between the work of the Unitarians and that of the Anglican Broad Churchmen in the nineteenth century.

But this affinity was not an entirely new phenomenon having no counterpart in the preceding century. Just as the Unitarian Church[2] emerged towards the end of the eighteenth century—the first church to be specifically designated "Unitarian" was opened in 1774,[3] and interestingly enough by a former Latitudinarian Anglican clergyman, Theophilus Lindsey—from a mainly English Presbyterian background, which exemplified in germ several of nineteenth-century Unitarianism's most characteristic features, so the Anglican Broad Church—which received the title "Broad" near the middle of the nineteenth century[4]—had its antecedents in the eighteenth century and earlier men of Latitude, as well as in the early nineteenth-century Noetics,[5] some of whom may also be described as Broad Churchmen; and between these groups there was a considerable measure of agreement.

It will be of assistance, therefore, both in the matter of general approach and of perspective, if, before the relations of nineteenth-century Unitarianism and Broad Church Anglicanism are considered, the most significant features that characterized the antecedents of both groups are set forth.

In the first place, both the English Presbyterians[6]—so called to distinguish them from the strict "Scottish" type Presbyterians who lacked their liberality of outlook—and the Latitudinarian Anglicans were tolerant in the matter of theological belief. The English Presbyterians, who, before the 1662 ejection had been "the most conservative and rigidly orthodox element in the Established Church",[7] had by the beginning of the eighteenth century achieved a much more liberal attitude. They held that Scripture only was the rule of faith, and this, with the right of private judgment, resulted in both variety and tolerance in matters of belief. They claimed, in the words of Timothy Jollie, the "liberty to reform according to Scripture rule in doctrine, discipline, and worship".[8] In spite of the fact that the Trinitarian controversy[9] arose during the period of their greatest activity in Church building, the English Presbyterians made no provision in their trust-deeds for the exclusion of heterodoxy, and their chapels were dedicated simply to "the worship of Almighty God",[10] without specific mention of the Trinity. Thus Francis Tallents when opening the new meeting house at Shrewsbury in 1691 "caused it to be written on the wall that it was built not for a faction or a party, but for the promotion of repentance and faith in communion with all that love the Lord Jesus Christ in sincerity".[11] In similar vein, Edmund Calamy, at his approach to ordination in 1694, declared that he must be ordained "Minister of the Catholic Church of Christ, without any confinement".[12] Still more strongly, Moses Lowman affirmed that "nothing is a more fundamental mistake in religion except what is inconsistent with a good heart and a religious conversation".[13] Later, Dr. John Taylor, though an Arian, is found declaring in a sermon preached in 1756: "We are Christians, and only Christians. . . . We disown all connection, except that of love and goodwill, with any sect or party whatever . . . so that we may exercise the public duties of Religion upon the most catholic and charitable foundation."[14] In the words of Richard Baxter, the English Presbyterians stood "for catholicism against parties".[15]

As already intimated the Latitudinarians held a similar view, their name, of course, being earned as a result of their broad tolerance in respect of doctrine and ecclesiastical organization. In the seventeenth century three scholars—Falkland, Hales and Chillingworth—stand out as being of particular importance. It was "very possibly at their instance"[16] that Acontius' *Satanae Strategemata* which pleaded for "a tolerance broad enough to unite all sects into a single church, holding doctrines that all Protestants own",[17] and "ignored as non-essential the Trinity, the deity of Christ, the Lord's Supper, and other hotly disputed doctrines",[18] was reprinted at Oxford in 1631. Writing of Falkland, John Tulloch says, "It seemed to him . . . possible to make room within the national Church for wide differences of dogmatic opinion",[19] and he notes that Falkland referred to "Constantine's famous letter on the Trinitarian controversy as showing that even on a question so great as this neither side was deemed without the pale of the Church".[20] Hales declared, "I do not yet see, that *opinionum varietas, et opinantium unitas*, are ἀσύστατα or that men of different opinions in Christian religion, may not hold communion *in sacris*, and both go to one Church. Why may I not go, if occasion require, to an Arian Church, so there be no Arianism expressed in their liturgy? And were liturgies and public forms of service so framed, as that they admitted not of particular and private fancies, but contained only such things, as in which all Christians do agree, schisms on opinion were utterly vanished."[21] The attitude of William Chillingworth, whose views "spread widely in the established Church", and so "contributed to create an atmosphere in which Unitarianism was soon to find an authentic voice and a numerous hearing",[22] may be seen from the following quotation: "I will take no man's liberty of judgment from him, neither shall any man take mine from me. I will think no man the worse man nor the worse Christian—I will love no man the less for differing in opinion from me; and what measure I mete to others I expect from them again. I am fully assured that God does not, and therefore that man ought not, to require any more of any man than this—to believe the Scripture to be God's word, to endeavour to find the true sense of it, and to live according to it."[23] Edward Stillingfleet, the Bishop of Worcester, held a similar view. Thus, in the *Irenicum* he wrote, "The unity of the Church is that of communion, and not that of apprehension; and different opinions are no further liable to censure than as men by the broaching of these do endeavour to disturb the peace of the Church."[24] It is only the "endeavour, by difference of opinion, to alienate men's spirit one from another, and thereby break the society into fractions and divisions, which makes men liable to restraint and punishment".[25] John Tillotson, later Archbishop of Canterbury, was while Dean of St. Paul's a member of the commission appointed in 1689 to form a Comprehension Scheme, and in his list of probable changes he included the rendering of all ceremonies indifferent and the revision of the liturgy so as to remove all ground of exception to it.[26] Further, during his incumbency of St. Lawrence Jewry, Unitarians were among the worshippers, and though he wrote against Socinianism, "the thought of excommunicating Thomas Firmin and his Unitarian friends was never for a moment entertained".[27]

Intimately connected with the foregoing was the dislike, on the part of both groups, of subscription to elaborate sets of articles of belief. Under the Toleration Act of 1689 English Presbyterian ministers were, of course, obliged to subscribe to the doctrinal articles of the Church of England. "In practice, however, this" was "evaded from a very early date."[28] Their attitude may be seen in the words of Richard Baxter: "We would have had the brethren to have offered to Parliament, the Apostles' Creed, the Lord's Prayer, and the Decalogue, as essentials or fundamentals which at least contain all that is necessary to salvation; . . . and whereas it is said 'a Socinian or a Papist will subscribe all this', I answered, 'so much the better, and so much the fitter it is to be a matter of our concord'."[29] Similarly John Humfrey wrote: "I am (I say) so far indeed of another mind that let Martin Luther say what he will and John Calvin say that he will; nay, the assembly of Divines, which is more, in their grave Confessions and Catechism, and more than that, let the Synod of Dort say also what it will, they are but men and I will not Captivate my Understanding to any of them. For this I am sure that all of them and I are out still in one thing or another, and will be so to the end of the World."[30] Further, when James Peirce, minister of a Presbyterian[31] Church at Exeter, was accused of spreading Arian views, and the matter came before the ministers of the Three Denominations[32] at the Salters' Hall Conference in 1719, an attempt was made to impose on all the ministers then present subscription to the first of the Thirty-nine Articles of the Church of England and the answers to the fifth and sixth questions of the Westminster Catechism. But the motion was opposed by the English Presbyterians as "involving the imposition of a creed which was inconsistent with the principles of Protestant Dissent";[33] and it was on this principle—not that of anti-Trinitarianism—that the motion was rejected. The same attitude is exhibited later still in Dr. John Taylor's words to his students at Warrington Academy: "I do solemnly charge you . . . That you admit, embrace, or assent to no principle, or sentiment, by me taught or advanced, but only so far as it shall appear to you to be supported and justified by proper evidence from Revelation or the reason of things. That you keep your mind always open to evidence. That you labour to banish from your breast all prejudice, prepossession or party zeal. That you study to live in peace and love with all your fellow Christians; and that you steadily assert for yourselves, and freely allow to others, the inalienable rights of judgment and conscience."[34]

A similar attitude was adopted by the Latitudinarians. Thus William Chillingworth wrote: "Take away this persecuting, burning, cursing, damning of men for not subscribing to the words of men as the words of God; require of Christians only to believe Christ and to call no man master but Him only; let those leave claiming infallibility that have no title to it, and let them that in their words disclaim it, disclaim it likewise in their actions; in a word, take away tyranny and restore Christians to the first full liberty of captivating their understanding to Scripture only."[35] Somewhat similarly Locke in his *Reasonableness of Christianity* contended that apart from belief in God, the only essential article of belief was the acknowledgement of Jesus as Messiah. "Nobody can add to these fundamental articles of faith, nor make any other necessary but what God hath made or declared to be so."[36] Further, in the latter half of the eighteenth century the Feathers Tavern Petition, organized by Francis Blackburne, Archdeacon of Cleveland, for the abolition of subscription to the Thirty-Nine Articles, was signed by nearly two hundred clergymen,[37] and received the approval, though not the signatures, of Edmund Law, Bishop of Carlisle, Richard Watson, Bishop of Llandaff, and William Paley, Archdeacon of Carlisle.[38] The petition came to nothing but is nevertheless indicative of a fairly widespread uneasiness regarding subscription to the Articles; and possibly more would have signed had they dared. E. M. Wilbur remarks that Theophilus Lindsey, who spent two or three months trying to collect signatures from the clergy, found that "many that were privately sympathetic and would have been glad to sign had they dared, were reluctant to give their superiors offence by public support".[39]

Besides being similar to each other in the foregoing matters of general principle, both groups were akin in the fact that, within them, heterodox opinions regarding the Trinity occurred. The Arianism which occasioned the decision of the Salters' Hall Conference in 1719 was not confined to James Peirce, and thereafter continued to spread among the English Presbyterians, until by 1770 only half of their congregations remained orthodox.[40] As the century drew to a close Arianism began to give way to actual Unitarian opinions.

Among the Latitudinarians heterodoxy in this regard was not without trace in the seventeenth century, but it was not until the eighteenth century that Arianism really raised its head. In this connection the two most important scholars were William Whiston, who, as a result of his Arian views, lost his chair of mathematics at Cambridge in 1710;[41] and Samuel Clarke, Chaplain to Queen Anne, and regarded as "the greatest English theologian of his time",[42] who in 1712 published his *The Scripture-doctrine of the Trinity* wherein he maintained that supreme worship was to be given to the Father alone, that Christ was to be worshipped only in a lower sense as Mediator, and that for the worship of the Holy Spirit there was no distinct warrant.[43] Bishop Hoadly, who during his lifetime exercised episcopal authority over four sees, held a similar view;[44] and in the prayers of his own composition which he appended to his *Plain Account of the Nature and End of the Lord's Supper*, which he published anonymously in 1733,[45] all the petitions are addressed to the Father alone.[46] The occurrence of Arianism in the Church of England in this period was sufficiently extensive to cause Daniel Waterland to publish at Cambridge in 1721 his *The Case of Arian Subscription Considered; and the several pleas and excuses for it particularly examined and confuted*. Indeed, Archbishop Wake (1657–1737) was driven to say, "some of our bishops are labouring to pull down the Church in which they minister, and to introduce such licentiousness as would overthrow the grace of the Holy Spirit, the Divinity of Christ, and all the fundamental articles of our religion".[47] One of his successors, however, Archbishop Herring (1693–1757), was sufficiently sympathetic in regard to Samuel Clarke's Arian revision of the *Book of Common Prayer* to be able to write of the book to Dr. John Jortin in 1753: "I have seen Dr. Clarke's Book of Common Prayer; I have read it, and approved the temper and wisdom of it; but into what times are we fallen, after so much light, and so much appearance of moderation that we can only *wish* for the success of truth. The world will not bear it."[48] In 1756 Bishop Clayton (1695–1758) of Clogher made a speech before the Irish House of Lords in favour of deleting from the liturgy the Nicene and Athanasian Creeds. His attacks on the doctrine of the Trinity continued for two more years until his death in 1758, when he was about to be prosecuted for heresy.[49] Similarly, Edmund Law, Bishop of Carlisle (1703–87), came to adopt an Arian position;[50] and it is probably not without significance that he "purged" the final edition of his *Considerations on the Theory of Religion* (1784) of the reference to the pre-existence of Christ which had occurred in earlier editions[51]—particularly as he drew attention to the fact in a letter[52] to Theophilus Lindsey, the Unitarian leader. The same year, viz., 1784,[53] saw the visit to England of La Rochefoucauld, who recorded of Anglican worshippers that "some . . . (and nearly all the women) refuse to accept the Trinity and shut their books when it occurs in the service".[54] Three years later Richard Watson, Bishop of Llandaff (1737–1816), recorded that he had avoided the use of the word "Trinity" in his divinity lectures at Cambridge,[55] and he added "let us not use unscriptural words to propagate unscriptural dogmas".[56] In 1790 he wrote: "We do not object to the doctrine of the Trinity because it is above our reason, and we cannot comprehend it, but we object to it because we cannot find that it is either literally contained in any passage of Holy Writ, or can by sound criticism be deduced from it";[57] and De Quincey, several years later, found that "he talked openly, at his own table, as a Socinian".[58] Other bishops considered to be more or less unsound on the Trinity were Thomas Rundle, Bishop of Derry, and Francis Hare, Bishop of Chichester.[59] In the same category should be placed such other distinguished clergy as William Paley,[60] and John Hey, the Norrisian Professor of Divinity at Cambridge, who declared: "We and the Socinians are said to differ about what? not about morality or natural religion, or the divine authority of the Christian religion; we differ only about what we do not understand; and about what is to be done on the part of God; and if we allowed each other to use expressions at will (and what great matter could be in what might almost be called unmeaning expressions?) we need never be upon our guard against each other."[61]

A few Latitudinarian clergy seceded from the Anglican Church on account of their heterodoxy and became avowed Unitarians. Here, of course, the chief name is Theophilus Lindsey, the founder of the first avowed Unitarian Church in 1774, followed by John Disney, who became his successor as minister of the Church in 1793, and John Jebb and William Frend,[62] both of whom became influential Unitarian laymen.

Evidence of mutual influence in the field of theological writing is also not wanting; and, among Latitudinarian writers, John Locke, Whiston, and Clarke stand out as having been especially influential in English Presbyterian circles. The writings of Locke—who himself had been influenced by the English Presbyterian, Richard Baxter[63]—had a great vogue among English Presbyterians. His *Letters Concerning Toleration* (1689, '90, '92), in which he pleaded for religious liberty for all except atheists and Roman Catholics, particularly endeared him to them.[64] His *Essay concerning Human Understanding* (1690) was for a long time used as a text in their academies,[65] and the view therein expressed that "man, by the right use of his natural abilities, may . . . attain a Knowledge of God" strengthened their belief in the right of private judgment.[66] His *Vindication of the Reasonableness of Christianity* argued for a reduction of the doctrinal essentials of Christianity to belief in the Messiahship of Jesus—which position was that of the majority of Unitarians before John James Tayler and James Martineau "changed the character and foundation of Unitarian doctrine".[67] Indeed, as late as 1851 the authority of Locke could be quoted by the *Christian Reformer*—representing the older type of Unitarian view—in support of an attack on Martineau for a sermon in which he declared that discussion of whether Jesus was the

Messiah was "unmeaning".[68] Locke's posthumous *A Paraphrase and Notes on the Epistles of St. Paul* (1705-7) became a model for the "older school of Unitarian hermeneutics".[69] Thus James Peirce's *Paraphrases and Notes of Paul's Epistles*, George Benson's *Paraphrases and Notes, Attempted in Mr. Locke's Manner*, John Taylor's *A Paraphrase with Notes on the Epistle to the Romans*, and Thomas Belsham's *Exposition of St. Paul's Epistles*, for example, all owed something to the influence of Locke.[70] The similarity of Locke's views to those of the Unitarians, coupled with his policy of writing anonymously, led to his being suspected of having contributed to the third volume of the *Unitarian Tracts*.[71]

William Whiston and Clarke—especially the latter—had an immense influence among the English Presbyterians. Indeed, the Arian movement among them may be said to have had its origin in their influence.[72] Whiston's *Primitive Christianity Revived* and Samuel Clarke's *Scripture-doctrine of the Trinity* were read secretly by many English Presbyterians at Exeter before the arrival of James Peirce, whose Arianism led to the Salters' Hall Controversy (1719);[73] and Peirce himself while minister at Cambridge had formed a close friendship with Whiston,[74] which doubtless affected his thinking. Clarke's *Scripture-doctrine of the Trinity* was eagerly read over a wide area, and much discussed in the Dissenting Academies.[75] Dr. John Taylor of Norwich read it with his congregation and the title of his own *The Scripture Doctrine of Original Sin* indicates something of his indebtedness to Clarke.[76] In a collection of brief biographical sketches entitled *Memorable Unitarians*, and published by the British and Foreign Unitarian Association in 1906, Clarke's book is described as "still one of the best text-books on the Unitarian controversy".[77]

Clarke's influence, however, was not limited to the *Scripture-doctrine of the Trinity*. He had a very important influence upon English Presbyterian and Unitarian liturgical practice. It was upon his revision of the Prayer Book that Theophilus Lindsey based the Prayer Book which he devised for use in Essex Street Chapel;[78] and between 1774 and 1791 no less than nine liturgies were published by the English Presbyterians—all but two of which having their basis in *The Book of Common Prayer* as annotated by Dr. Samuel Clarke.[79]

In less spectacular ways, too, Latitudinarian theological writings had their influence. Thus, for example, a copy of Archbishop Tillotson's sermons was kept at Lydgate Chapel, Huddersfield, for use when a minister was not available to preach;[80] and Bishop Law's *Reflections on the Life and Character of Christ* featured as a tract circulated by the Unitarian Society.[81]

English Presbyterian or Unitarian theological writings were similarly appreciated, and, perhaps to a somewhat smaller extent, influential in Latitudinarian circles. Thus Tillotson, though preaching against Socinianism, admitted in respect of Unitarian tract writers "that generally they are a pattern of the fair way of disputing and debating matters of religion without heat and unseemly reflections upon their adversaries . . . and for the most part they reason closely and clearly, with great dexterity and decency".[82] In the list of commentators on the New Testament recommended by William Paley to his students at Cambridge no less than four—James Peirce, Joseph Hallet, George Benson, and John Taylor—of the five given were heterodox Dissenters.[83] Nathaniel Lardner's *Credibility of the Gospel History* was the main source for Paley's famous *Evidences of Christianity*, Paley having but to "select and polish the weapons" provided in Lardner's "antiquarian armoury".[84] Both Lardner's *A History of the Apostles and Evangelists, writers of the New Testament* and his *Of the argument for the Truth of Christianity* appeared in Bishop Watson's *Collection of Theological Tracts*, as did Samuel Chandler's *Plain Reasons for being a Christian*, together with three extracts from George Benson's *Paraphrase and Notes on St. Paul's Epistles* and John Taylor's *Key to the Apostolic Writings* and *Scheme of Scripture-Divinity*.

In a letter to Theophilus Lindsey regarding the printing of Joseph Priestley's *Church History* and *Notes on the Scriptures* John Law, the Bishop of Elphin, wrote in 1802: "Enclosed is a draft for one hundred pounds, which you will apply in aid of Dr. Priestley's publication . . . but my name must on no account be mentioned . . . as it would involve me with some acquaintance here, and do me more mischief than you can imagine";[85] and several years earlier the writer's father, Bishop Edmund Law, had, in a letter to the same recipient regarding his *An Historical View of the State of Unitarian Doctrine and Worship from the Reformation to our own Times*, written: "I received the favour of your *Historical View*, and read it with satisfaction. You appear to have cleared up all the passages of Scripture usually alleged in favour of the contrary opinion, and to have exhausted the subject. . . . That all the success and satisfaction may attend your labours to which you are so justly entitled is the most hearty wish of your sincere friend and servant."[86]

The affinity which has thus far been broadly sketched between the English Presbyterians and the Latitudinarians can, as has already been stated, be paralleled in the nineteenth century, and, since the topic of theological writings has been raised, it will be appropriate to begin in the next chapter with an account of the affinity which existed between the nineteenth-century representatives of both groups in the matter of approach to Biblical study. Before this is undertaken, however, it is necessary that a few words be added with regard to both the Anglican Broad Church and nineteenth-century Unitarianism.

The Broad Church received its name, as has already been indicated, about the middle of the nineteenth century, but facts come before names, and largely in the group of Anglicans known as Noetics—Richard Whately, Thomas Arnold and Baden Powell, for example—who, in their critical and liberal attitude, exhibited something of the spirit of the Latitudinarians, the Broad Church, before it received its name, had its existence; and most of the Noetics have, at one time or another, and with good reason, been termed "Broad Churchmen".[87] The latter, of course, did not exhibit a solid, uniform body of religious opinion. Within the Broad Church many shades of opinion were to be found. F. D. Maurice, for example, who in spite of his own protestations, is generally classed with the Broad Churchmen, represented a much more conservative position generally than did, say, Dean Stanley, or, yet more strongly, Charles Voysey; and this must be borne in mind in the following study, for it is—insofar as the distinction made by F. W. Cornish is valid—with the "critical or historical" section of the Broad Church, as opposed to the "philosophical",[88] represented by Maurice, that the present study is in the main concerned, though, even here, it will be seen, nevertheless, that some affinity with Unitarianism may be discerned.

Rather curiously, a somewhat similar division may be observed in the Unitarianism of the nineteenth century. On the one hand, there was the more conservative, Biblically based, and denominationally inclined wing, represented by such men as Robert Aspland and Samuel Bache; and on the other hand, the liberal, and finally more dominant wing, represented by John James Tayler and James Martineau, which recognized supreme authority not in Scripture but in reason, conscience and the soul, and, in accordance with its English Presbyterian heritage, stood for a generous breadth in the sphere of doctrine.[89] It is with this wing that the following pages are in the main concerned.

CHAPTER 2

The Affinity shown in the Approach to Higher Criticism

The acceptance of, and contribution to, higher criticism constituted, in the first sixty or so years of the period, a noteworthy,
and almost unique, point of affinity between the Anglican
Broad Church and the Unitarian movement in the nineteenth
century. On the Continent considerable advances were made
in higher criticism; but, in England, a number of factors, including clerical ignorance of German,[1] suspicion regarding new
ideas, and, above all, the widespread acceptance of the verbal
and superintendence theories of Biblical inspiration—according
to which all statements in the Bible, whether concerning science,
history or religion were sacrosanct—made progress in this subject slow during the first half of the century.[2] The English Nonconformist churches, for the most part tenaciously conservative,
made but little contribution. Thus it was not until 1856 that
Samuel Davidson's rather tentative espousal of higher criticism
was published, and this "heresy" cost him his Professorship at
the Lancashire Independent College in the following year.[3] And
in the Anglican Church both Tractarian and Evangelical regarded with apprehension such progress as was effected within
their own church.[4] Indeed, it may be said that higher criticism
did not receive approval within the Anglican Church until the
middle sixties, after the Broad Churchmen, in the persons of the
contributors to *Essays and Reviews* had publicly challenged
orthodox vigilance and the resultant "unwholesome reticence
of the clergy"[5] by deciding, in the words of Professor Jowett,
"not to submit to this abominable system of terrorism which
prevents the statement of the plainest facts and makes true
theology or theological education impossible".[6] Progress, how-

ever, was made in England in this period, and that largely as a result of the labours of Unitarians and Broad Churchmen.

At the beginning of the century Unitarians shared the common attitude to the Bible in regarding it as a unique revelation and storehouse of doctrine. Thus Timothy Kenrick in his *Address to Young Men* (1795) wrote, "Let it be your endeavour to obtain the divine will in the purest state, from the only authentic record of it contained in the Bible";[7] and Charles Wellbeloved, Principal of Manchester College, declared in 1823, in a controversy with Archdeacon Wrangham, "I adopt the common language of Unitarians when I say, 'Convince us that any tenet is authorized by the Bible, from that moment we receive it.' "[8] Their rationalistic approach, however, caused some Unitarians to reject parts of Scripture as interpolations, as when, for example, Timothy Kenrick in his *Exposition of the Historical Writings of the New Testament* (1807) made no reference to the opening chapters of Matthew and Luke, because, in the words of his editor, "he did not look upon the chapters in question as the production of those evangelists, but as fabrications by an unknown, though early, hand".[9] This, of course, along with the familiarity with Continental scholarship, which some of their ministers possessed as a result of training in Germany,[10] placed Unitarians in a leading position in the matter of higher criticism among Nonconformists in England during the first sixty years or so of the century.

Only eight years before the century began, the Unitarian scholar, Edward Evanson, who, interestingly enough, until his resignation in 1778 had been a Latitudinarian clergyman in the Church of England, reached extremely radical, and decidedly eccentric, conclusions in his *The Dissonance of the Four Generally Received Evangelists, and the Evidence of their Respective Authenticity Examined* (1792). The fairly common false ascription of apostolic authorship to various non-apostolic books in the second century, by writers of that period, made suspect, he believed, the authorship of the Gospels, since their traditional authorship rested on second-century testimony; and the criterion by which he thought revelation should be determined, viz., the fulfilment of prophecy,[11] along with other more critical determinants regarding the matter of dating, such as his curious view that the use of Latin words spelled with Greek letters in place of Greek words indicates second-century authorship,[12] led him to reject as unauthentic Matthew, Mark, and John, which latter he considered to be the work of "a convert of the second century from the Platonic school".[13] In his attack on the apostolic authorship of the Fourth Gospel, Evanson, of course, raised a matter which had lain dormant since the time of the Alogi, and anticipated by nearly thirty years the abler work of Bretschneider in 1820.

Other criticisms—as, for example, in the case of Romans, the fact that the epistle represents the Church in Rome as being known throughout the world, whereas in Acts no such church is known when Paul arrives there[14]—led him to the extremely drastic rejection of Romans, Ephesians, Colossians, Hebrews, and the epistles of James, John, and Jude; and his *New Testament*, published in 1807, two years after his death, was even more truncated than that of Marcion. Though Evanson's views are now in the category of "critical curiosities", H. McLachlan rightly remarks that, "as a pioneer in the comparative study of the Gospels", Evanson has nevertheless, "secured a place for himself in the history of New Testament criticism".[15]

In contrast with Evanson's assessment, Thomas Belsham, in his *A Summary View of the Evidence and Practical Importance of the Christian Revelation* (1807) held that "the books of the New Testament are in the main genuine".[16] Belsham, of course, was the principal editor of *The Improved Version of the New Testament* (1808), the preface to which presented a valuable summary of the history of the canon and text, the versions and editions, along with a brief discussion of the use of critical conjecture, etc., which discussion was described by a contemporary reviewer as "the best compend of criticism respecting the state of the Greek text, which has yet been presented to the English reader".[17] The version itself anticipated many of the judgments adopted in the *Revised Version* of 1881, and, moreover, as Alexander Gordon has remarked, "its endeavour to exhibit typographically distinct strata in the Gospels, if a crude initial effort, was nevertheless a suggestive beginning".[18] Belsham's alertness to New Testament problems is revealed in a letter written to John Kenrick in 1819. "I love", he writes, "German criticism as much as I dislike German theology . . . I think the origin of the four evangelists is a very great difficulty. If the four histories existed in their present form in the time of Justin Martyr, it is most unaccountable that he should never quote them by name . . . I suspect that the number was never fixed to four till Irenaeus made the notable discovery that there must be four Gospels, and no more, because there are four winds. . . . Still, however, the main part of the respective Gospels must have been written by the authors to whom they are attributed, otherwise, how could the whole Christian world be so unanimous in ascribing them to those authors? But before they were universally known and acknowledged, I am inclined to believe that those who were in possession of early copies made additions of narratives, which they believed to be authentic."[19] Shrewdly, indeed, very shrewdly for that period in England, Belsham adds "and it seems that Matthew has been more corrupted than any of the rest; and Mark, perhaps, the least, because of its brevity".[20] In his *Exposition of St. Paul's Epistles* (1822) he enunciated the important principle that "an Expositor will not feel himself bound to warp and strain a text from its plain and obvious meaning because that meaning is erroneous, and to adopt some unusual and far-fetched interpretation in order to reconcile it to the truth, because, at all events, the proposition must be justified; but he will endeavour to find out the true meaning of the author, according to the established and approved rules of interpretation, leaving the whole responsibility, whether for the sense, the truth, or the reasoning of the passage, upon the author himself, without any pain for the result".[21]

In the study of the Old Testament Belsham was influenced by Astruc, Geddes, and Eichhorn; and in 1807—only four years after Priestley had written "I see no reason to entertain a doubt of Moses being the writer of the first five books of the Old

Testament"[22]—Belsham took the then revolutionary step of drawing attention to the composite nature of the Pentateuch.[23] Several years later, in a sermon preached at Warrington in 1821, he rejected the Mosaic authorship of Genesis, declaring, furthermore, "If the history of the creation in the first chapter of Genesis be inspired, then all the discoveries of Kepler and Galileo, of Copernicus and Newton, are false, and all their demonstrations must be erroneous, which is impossible."[24] "The humble and sincere inquirer after truth", he urged, should "read the Scriptures of the Old and New Testaments with the same thirst after knowledge, and with the same liberal and candid spirit with which he would read any other ancient volume",[25] and thus he adopted a position identical with that of Benjamin Jowett, when, in 1860, the latter declared that the interpreter's object should be "to read Scripture like any other book, with a real interest and not merely a conventional one".[26]

In 1838 Charles C. Hennell, a Unitarian layman, published his *Inquiry concerning the Origin of Christianity*. Though he received no formal theological education and knew very little of what had been done in Germany,[27] he enunciated principles for the study of the Gospels which have, in fact, governed the approach of most critical scholarship in more recent times. Thus he wrote: "It is necessary to form an opinion as to the date of each writing, the general character of each author, his peculiarities as a writer; to institute continual comparisons between the events or controversies which arose subsequently to his own time; to weigh the probability in favour of the real occurrence of a fact, considered in reference to the ascertained history of the time, with that in favour of its invention by the author or some intermediate narrator; to consider what greater degree of weight is due to the testimony from the accordance of all, or of several of the writers; and to ascertain whether they wrote independently or copied from each other."[28]

The first Gospel, he decided, in view of such characteristics, as, for example, the absence of such details as an eye-witness would give, was not the work of Matthew, the Apostle, but the product of a member of the Jewish Church "who collected relics of the acts and sayings of Jesus reported by Matthew, the Apostle, introducing some traditions which he found elsewhere, and filling up copiously from his own imagination"[29] as when, for example, he modifies a story to make it correspond more closely with Old Testament prophecy.[30] The second Gospel, he considered, was written by Mark, "the epitomizer of Matthew",[31] who, however, in separate stories had amplified his original "so as to render it more exact and forcible".[32] Such Matthean narratives as the stories of the dream of Pilate's wife and the resurrection of the saints, were omitted by Mark "because he did not believe them and did not expect to be believed if he related them".[33] The third Gospel, he thought, was the composition of Luke, who may have been identical with Silas,[34] and who drew largely from Matthew and Mark, especially the latter, as well as from other sources. That the Lucan order of events, after the first few chapters, is less reliable than that of Matthew is shown by the inappropriateness of the context for some of the sayings.[35] The fourth Gospel, he observed, is clearly marked off from the other Gospels both by the style of its discourses and by its subject matter;[36] and between it and the Synoptics "there are many glaring inconsistencies in its order and description of events".[37] The character of Jesus has undergone some idealization.[38] Hennell, however, though he is suspicious regarding the historicity of the fourth Gospel, does not deny its connection with John the Apostle, and expresses the opinion that the greater part of the book was either written or dictated by the Apostle a few years before the close of the first century and for the use of the Ephesian Church.[39]

Though Hennell is primarily concerned with the New Testament, it is possible to gather from the *Inquiry* some of his views regarding the Old Testament. Thus he thinks that "there are many indications that the Pentateuch was compiled by Samuel";[40] that Daniel is the product of the time of Antiochus Epiphanes;[41] and that though the first thirty-nine chapters of Isaiah "contain much that was probably written by Isaiah himself",[42] the rest of the book is the work of a patriotic

Israelite about the time of the return of the Babylonian captivity.

Though Hennell wished his book to be regarded as "employed in the real service of Christianity rather than as an attack on it",[43] and his tone is reverent, the *Inquiry* is very rationalistic—the disciples' belief in the physical resurrection of Jesus, for example, is regarded as being a consequence of Joseph of Arimathea's secret removal of the body from the tomb in his garden in order to deflect from himself the unwanted attention of the Jewish authorities[44]—and there can be small doubt that Hennell's book contributed not a little to that unsettlement of belief which occasioned for many the adoption of Broad Church views.[45]

In 1847 Francis W. Newman published his *The Hebrew Monarchy*, a work which though not professedly concerned with higher criticism is yet based upon such an approach. The writer does not "pretend to an exhaustive German erudition",[46] but is familiar with the work of De Wette, Hitzig, and Ewald. Deuteronomy, he gives reasons for thinking, was only recently produced in the time of Josiah,[47] about which time also Exodus, Leviticus and Numbers took their final shape.[48] Like Genesis the latter are "piece-meal works, made up out of pre-existing fragments, which are duplicate accounts of similar events or laws, and often mutually inconsistent".[49] The candid spirit of the book may be judged from the fact that it refers to the anointing of David at Bethlehem as "that which is politically called treason".[50]

In an article mistitled "The Relation of the Third to the First Two Gospels", which appeared in the *Prospective Review* (1850), John Kenrick, the Principal of Manchester College, argued for the priority of Mark[51] and principally on the grounds of its greater vividness, which he took to indicate the lively memory of recent events;[52] the absence of the exaggeration which may be seen in Matthew; and its plainness and freedom in the use of expressions which the other authors avoided lest they should seem to derogate from the character of Jesus. Though he declares at the outset that he is not concerned to discuss the origin of the verbal similarities between the three Gospels, Kenrick yet expresses dissatisfaction with the theories of J. G. Eichhorn, Herbert Marsh, and Andrews Norton,[53] and observes that the priority of Mark will go far to suggest that Matthew and Luke made borrowings. Rather curiously Kenrick thinks that Mark is more of a private record of facts than a book written for the public. In the course of the article he declares that "we must deal with the evangelists as human biographers, not only possessing no supernatural source of knowledge, nor guarded from error by any divine superintendence, but men of 'like infirmities with ourselves' and exposed to the influences of their age, their country, and their family connections"[54]—an advanced position for the middle of the nineteenth century.[55]

In 1851 William R. Greg, a Unitarian layman, published his *The Creed of Christendom*, a powerful book in which he attempted to establish "that the tenet of Inspiration of the Scriptures is baseless and untenable under any form or modification which leaves it a dogmatic value; that the Gospels are not textually faithful records of the sayings and actions of Jesus, but ascribe to him words which he never uttered, and deeds which he never did; and that the Apostles only partially comprehended, and imperfectly transmitted, the teaching of their Great Master".[56]

The book reveals a considerable acquaintance with German scholarship, and the author accepts the theory of De Wette that "the Book of Deuteronomy was written about the time of Josiah, shortly before, and with a view to, the discovery of the Pentateuch in the Temple".[57] Two principal documents—the Elohistic, dating from the time of Saul, and the Jehovistic, dating from the period of Solomon—he considered made up the remaining books of the Pentateuch, "which assumed its present form about the reign of Josiah, B.C. 624".[58] Accepting the theory expressed by the Unitarian scholar, Kenrick, in his *Essay on Primaeval History*, Greg thinks that the first eleven chapters of Genesis are not "tradition handed down from the earliest times concerning the primitive conditions of the human race, and the immediate ancestors of the Jewish nation", but simply "speculations, originally framed to account for existing facts and appearances", such as, for example, the different languages of the nations, which speculations "by the lapse of time gradually hardened into narrative".[59] As to other books of the Old Testament, Greg dates Kings at "near the termination of the Babylonian Exile",[60] and Chronicles between 400 and 260 B.C.[61] The last twenty-seven chapters of Isaiah, he thinks, were composed during the Babylonian Captivity,[62] and Daniel was a product of the time of Antiochus Epiphanes.[63]

On turning to the New Testament Greg finds that Matthew is not the book stated by Papias and others to have been written in Hebrew, for this Gospel is written in Greek, and "learned men are satisfied from internal evidence that it is not a translation".[64] The occurrence of double narratives, which "indicate the confusion of a man who was compiling from fragmentary materials rather than the fulness and clearness of personal recollection",[65] as well as other internal characteristics, show that Matthew is not the work of an eye-witness, and the latter statement applies also to Luke and Mark. The latter he regards, with Kenrick, as being the earliest Gospel, but the fact that Mark was a common Roman name renders the connection of the book with Mark of the Acts somewhat dubious. On the question of the authorship of the Fourth Gospel, in view of the strength of the arguments on both sides, he finds it impossible to decide;[66] but the fact that the Fourth Gospel makes no reference to such events as the raising of Jairus' daughter, at which the Synoptics represent John as being present, must mean, he thinks, that either the Fourth Gospel was not written by John or that the Synoptics' accounts of the events were not genuine.[67] As to the origin of the Synoptics, he rejects both the theory of an *Urevangelium* and the view that one evangelist wrote first and that the others copied from him, but accepts the theory first propounded by Lessing, and later revived and modified by Schleiermacher, that the Gospels were composed from a number of fragmentary oral and written narratives.[68]

Like Hennell's *Inquiry*, Greg's *Creed* had its share in the creation of that unsettlement of traditional beliefs which resulted for many in the development of Broad Church opinions. Referring to *The Creed of Christendom* John Morley remarked, "It is enough ... to remind ourselves how serious a place is held by that work in the dissolvent literature of the generation. The present writer was at Oxford in the last three years of the decade in which it appeared, and can well recall the share that it had, along with Mansel's *Bampton Lectures* and other books on both sides, in shaking the fabric of early beliefs in some of the most active minds then in the University. The landmarks have so shifted within the last twenty years that the *Creed of Christendom* is now comparatively orthodox. But in those days it was a remarkable proof of intellectual courage and independence to venture on introducing to the English public the best results of German theological criticism, with fresh applications from an original mind."[69]

In 1853 Edward Higginson, the brother-in-law of James Martineau, and himself a minister, published *The Spirit of the Bible, or the Nature and Value of the Jewish and Christian Scriptures Discriminated*. Though the two volumes are "not addressed to the professional student of critical theology"[70] but to the general reader, Higginson's purpose is "to give something of methodical expression to the growing opinion and faith of intelligent readers of the Bible—of such as do not timidly suppress their scriptural doubts and difficulties, but reverently think them out",[71] and the book, in spite of its conservatism[72] in comparison with some of the foregoing, nevertheless gives expression to a number of interesting critical opinions.

The existence of Elohistic and Jehovistic strands is recognized in Genesis,[73] but the view that the Pentateuch took its final form in the time of Josiah or Ezra, Higginson rejects on the ground that in that case the priests would have given the material more symmetrical form.[74] The lack of order or "half-journal like form" is accounted for "if these laws were, in part at least, written down by Moses, or under his direction, at or near the time when he gave them as circumstances called for them".[75] Hence Higginson thinks that the basis of the Pentateuch was "put into writing by Moses, or under his direction".[76]

He observes that the traditional ascription of Ecclesiastes to Solomon is "called in question by some of the best critics, who ascribe the book to a decidedly later period of Jewish literature".[77] The first words of the Song of Solomon may mean either "A most excellent song by Solomon" or "A most excellent song about Solomon". It is not a religious book, but "plainly an amatory poem or a series of such poems".[78] Jonah, he thinks, is "a moral tale" and is "not to be taken for a true story".[79] Isaiah cc. 40–66 were not the product of Isaiah of Jerusalem, but the "work of a later prophet who lived during the capitivity and return,—a prophet probably of the same name, certainly of kindred genius, whom we may call 'the second Isaiah' ";[80] and by the "Servant" in Chapter 53 the prophet did not mean Jesus Christ, but "the redeemed Israelitish nation".[81] Daniel, Higginson decides, after a fairly full discussion, belongs to the time of Antiochus Epiphanes.[82]

On turning to the New Testament he accepts Kenrick's view that Mark's Gospel was the first to be written and that it may have been seen by the other evangelists. He accepts the traditional authorship of Matthew, but refers to the stories of Herod and the Wise Men as having "a somewhat Apocryphal air",[83] and, of the reference to the raising of the saints in the crucifixion story, says, "We are strongly tempted to conjecture that a legend to this effect has crept into Matthew's Gospel with no sufficient authority."[84] The Fourth Gospel, he thinks, was composed by John, but remarks that the "conversations and discourses cannot, of course, be taken to be verbatim and literatim as our Lord spoke them".[85] On the subject of the authorship of Hebrews he considers that it was not by Paul, but that little can be added to the judgment of Origen. 2 Peter and Jude are of dubious authenticity; and the literary style of Revelation shows that it did not proceed from the same hand as the Fourth Gospel and the Johannine Epistles.[86]

In 1857 George Vance Smith published a linguistic and exegetical commentary entitled *The Prophecies Relating to Nineveh and the Assyrians*. The book provides an independent translation, notes recent archaeological discoveries, and shows the influence of Gesenius, Ewald, Knobel, Hitzig and Otto Strauss. It deals mainly with the first thirty-nine chapters of Isaiah, and an attempt is made to arrange them in chronological sequence. Jonah is treated as a moral tale.[87] Significantly, Smith remarks that it is "a great mistake to suppose . . . that the prophets were solely or mainly occupied with predictions relating to the distant future. On the contrary . . . they were intimately concerned with the affairs of their own day, and exercised often a powerful influence upon them".[88]

In 1867 John James Tayler published his *Attempt to Ascertain the Character of the Fourth Gospel, especially in its Relation to the Three First*. The book, which reveals Tubingen influence, is important as being the first full-scale statement in English of the case against the traditional authorship.[89] Drawing attention to the numerous features which distinguish the Fourth Gospel from the Synoptics, Tayler remarks that "John's is not so much another, as in one sense a different Gospel".[90]

Between the Fourth Gospel and Revelation there are important differences in style and spirit, so much so, indeed, that both cannot have proceeded from the same hand.[91] But both the character of Revelation and the testimony of antiquity point to Johannine authorship of the Apocalypse which means that the Fourth Gospel cannot be the work of John the Apostle.[92] Moreover, the internal character of the Fourth Gospel, for example, the Logos doctrine of which there is only an 'incipient trace" in Paul, and the mystical interpretation of the Lord's Supper, points to a late date.[93]

As to precise dating and authorship Tayler confesses his inability to give a categorical answer. But the signs in the Gospel that the church had made a final breach with Judaism, he thinks, suggests a period subsequent to A.D. 135, when the revolt of Bar Cochba—during which Christians had been persecuted by Jews—had finally been put down;[94] and the fact that the Second and Third Epistles—which in language and style closely resemble the First, the author of which latter was almost certainly that of the Gospel—have in their heading the title "Presbyter" suggests that the author of the Fourth Gospel may have been John, the Presbyter of Ephesus, referred to by Eusebius.[95]

The foregoing survey will have shown something of the extent to which Unitarians contributed to higher criticism during the first sixty years or so of the nineteenth century; and it is not proposed to continue this survey beyond the present point, for, while it may be true that "at the mid century only the more advanced Unitarians were ready to adopt German criticism",[96] and the *British Weekly* could say regarding higher criticism as late as 1887 that "except among the Unitarians, who boast some admirable Hebrew scholars, a profound ignorance prevails in this country",[97] yet the fact remains that the acceptance of higher criticism was not something peculiar to Unitarianism or to the Anglican Broad Church in the later period and was becoming characteristic of the wider body of English churches, so much so that "before the 'nineties were half over the prevalence of a critical view of the Bible among all the major nonconformist bodies was assured".[98]

Although as W. B. Glover has said, "The first important espousal of higher criticism by the Anglican Broad Church was in *Essays and Reviews* in 1860,"[99] the importance of the espousal lay far less in its intrinsic nature as criticism than in its effect in precipitating an ecclesiastical crisis and the consequent establishment of the legitimacy of liberal views within the Anglican Church.[100] Glover's remark regarding the writers in *Essays and Reviews*, viz., that they "show themselves in sympathy with the naturalistic approach to Christianity and the Bible which was the orientation of most higher critics of the century"[101] could certainly be used of other earlier members of the Broad Church school than the writers he mentions.[102] Furthermore, while it is true that the number of books by Broad Church writers during the first sixty years or so of the century which could be termed works of higher criticism in the strictest sense is very small, yet the fact remains that the Broad Churchmen did produce a number of books which contain the elements of such criticism— and which, moreover, cannot be significantly paralleled in any other section of the English Church in that period, except among

40

the Unitarians. Such facts as these indicate a significant similarity of approach between Broad Church writers and Unitarians.

It remains to give some indication of the Broad Church contribution towards higher criticism during the period under discussion. Not a few of the writers, it will be seen, were Noetics, having connections with Oriel College.[103]

In his Warburtonian Lectures on the *Nature and History of Prophecy* (1819–20) John Davison, Fellow of Oriel, took an important step towards the creation of a more intelligent appreciation of Old Testament prophecy. Opposing the interpretation of prophecy in the light of pre-conceived notions of its nature, he boldly declared: "By examining the actual contents of prophecy, we shall take the only legitimate method of investigating its use. For our duty is not to assign to it such a character as we might think it ought to have, and to read it to find that character: but to follow its course and reason, and thereby inform ourselves what was the mission of the prophet, and what the purport and end of his prophecy. A restriction this to which we must submit, whatever be our doubt or unbelief. . . ."[104] Against the prevailing mode of interpretation he contended that "what is merely ingenious or subtle in the exposition of prophecy has little chance of being useful or true";[105] and condemned the "mistaken principle which has infinitely warped the interpretation of it, in the hands of persons of an excellent piety, but an ill-instructed judgment; the principle of endeavouring to expound almost every prophecy, either immediately or typically, in a Christian sense".[106] Furthermore, though he allowed a greater predictive element to prophecy than later scholarship was able to confirm, he yet declared that "prophecy . . . is not a series of mere predictions",[107] and placed a much-needed emphasis on the moral content of prophecy and the related fact that the prophet was a religious teacher with a message for his own age. Davison was not strictly a higher critic, however, and he accepted, for example, the traditional view that the Prophets were written subsequently to the Law;[108] but his treatment of prophecy pointed the way for others, who went farther along the road than he.

In 1825 Connop Thirlwall, Cambridge scholar, and later Bishop of St. David's—who, like H. H. Milman, may be classed as a Noetic[109]—took the important step of publishing, though anonymously, Schleiermacher's *A Critical Essay on the Gospel of Luke*, wherein was set forth the thesis that the Gospels were composed from detached fragmentary narratives written beforehand. In the lengthy introduction in which he recounted the progress of the debate since the beginning of the century regarding the origin of the Synoptic Gospels, Thirlwall defended the principles of Schleiermacher's Biblical criticism, and rejected the popular theory of mechanical inspiration.

In 1828 Richard Whately, one of the most distinguished sons of Oriel, and later Archbishop of Dublin, published his *Essays on Some Difficulties in the Writings of St. Paul*, which, though strictly not a work of higher criticism, was of value in promoting a more intelligent and critical study of Scripture. Rejecting the plenary inspiration of Scripture as erroneous, he believed that some who upheld it did so from prudential motives.

In his approach to the study of Scripture the student must maintain an unbiased mind,[110] and be uninfluenced either by the desire for originality[111] or by undue respect for "venerated authority".[112] For the correct interpretation of Scripture a text must not be considered "as an insulated proposition",[113] instead "the general drift and design"[114] of each writer must be taken into account. Furthermore, affirms Whately, "there is . . . no more fruitful source of error . . . than the principle of interpreting Scripture on the principles of a scientific system, and endeavouring to make out, as in mathematics, a complete technical vocabulary, with precise definitions of all the terms employed such as may be applied in every case where they occur. Nothing manifestly was further from the design of the Sacred Writers, than to frame any such system: their writings were popular, not scientific; they expressed their meaning, on each occasion, in the terms which on each occasion suggested themselves as best fitted to convey it; and he who would interpret rightly each of these terms, must interpret it in each passage according to the context of the place where it is found".[115] Perhaps, however, nothing can better convey Whately's approach to the Bible than the following quotation from the same work: "We must not imitate the bigotted papists who imprisoned Galileo; and step forward Bible in hand, (like the profane Israelites carrying the ark of God into the field of battle) to check the inquiries of the geologist, the astronomer, or the political economist, from the apprehension that the cause of religion can be endangered by them."[116] Writing in 1893, an octogenarian Unitarian minister, Henry Solly, declared of Whately: "The present generation is hardly aware of what the Christian Church and the cause of an enlightened scriptural theology owe to the life and labours of this brave and earnest fellow-student and contemporary of Dr. Arnold, with his keen incisive intellect, and his fearless devotedness to truth."[117]

In the following year Henry H. Milman, later Dean of St. Paul's, published his *History of the Jews*, which, because of its critical character, aroused such anger that *The Family Library*, the series in which it appeared, was forced to discontinue. The work, of course, is not one of higher criticism, and no notice is taken of the various literary strata that went into the composition of the Pentateuch. Nevertheless, an essentially critical attitude is adopted, and the Biblical narratives are subjected to the same treatment as would be accorded to the historical traditions of any other ancient people. Numerical and chronological difficulties are clearly acknowledged, and certain narratives explained as oriental poetry and allegory. A naturalistic interpretation, furthermore, is given of numerous miraculous, or *prima facie* miraculous events. Thus, the sweetening of the waters of Marah by Moses' introduction of a branch may have been the result of the action of oxalic acid in the latter upon calcium sulphate in the water;[118] the destruction of Sennacherib's army by an angel is likely to have been really the work of "the Simoon or hot pestilential wind of the desert which is said not infrequently to have been fatal to whole caravans";[119] and of the backward movement of the shadow on Ahaz's dial, Milman remarks: "It is not necessary to suppose that the sun actually receded, but that the shadow on the dial did; a phenomenon which might be caused by a cloud refracting the light."[120]

Though Milman would not seem very radical today, such was not the case when he wrote; and by writing *The History of the Jews* he did not a little towards the creation of a freer attitude towards the Bible and its study, Dean Stanley, in fact, describing it as "the first decisive inroad of German theology into England, the first palpable indication that the Bible could be studied like another book, that the characters and events of the sacred history could be treated at once both critically and reverently".[121]

In 1831 Thomas Arnold, the most famous member of the Oriel school, published his *Essay on the Right Interpretation and Understanding of Scripture*, in which he made some application of the principles of historical criticism that he had learned from Niebuhr. Though, according to today's standards, the work is far from advanced in the nature of its views, "the objections which this Essay excited at the time in various quarters were very great".[122]

The Bible, Arnold insists, is not to be treated like the Koran, each passage having equal authority, for it is the product of different periods, and each figure and item must be considered in the light of its historical setting. Thus, for example, Abraham's attempted sacrifice of Isaac must be judged in the light of the then prevailing customs and conditions.[123]

Arnold, furthermore, made a distinction between the truth of the Bible and the inspiration of the historical record. Thus he maintains "first that by far the greatest part of the objections, not of a religious character which have been brought against the Scriptures, affect *the inspiration of the historical books*, and that only. And secondly that the *credibility* of these books does in no way depend upon their *inspiration*".[124] Moreover, though Arnold admits that "as things now are, a man cannot prosecute a critical inquiry as to the date and authorship of the books of scripture, without fear of having his christian faith impeached, should his conclusions in any instance be at variance with the common opinion",[125] he insists on reason's being given the right to exercise its sway. Thus, of "intellectual wisdom" he maintains: "It is within her province to judge all questions of science, of history and of criticism, according to her general laws; nor may her decisions on these matters be disputed by an appeal to the higher power of spiritual wisdom, who leaves such points wholly to her lower jurisdiction."[126] In consequence, all the aids of historical and critical knowledge, including the study of Hebrew, neglect of which in this country he deeply regretted,[127] must be brought to bear in the interpretation of Scripture. "Even in the last year of his life", his biographer records, Arnold "said that he looked upon it (the *Essay*) as the most important thing he had ever written";[128] and subsequent scholarship has confirmed this judgment. Thus, R. J. Campbell records: "All competent students of English history in the early nineteenth century are agreed that the field of Arnold's most lasting influence was that of the rational interpretation of scripture."[129]

But Arnold's activity in this matter was not confined to the foregoing essay. Thus in 1839 he published *Two Sermons on the Interpretation of Prophecy*, wherein he showed that often supposedly Christian prophecies in the Old Testament "do not relate to the Messiah or to Christian times, but are either the expression of religious affections generally, such as submission, hope, love, etc., or else refer to some particular circumstances in the life and condition of the writer, or the Jewish nation";[130] and in 1840, in a letter to Sir Thomas Pasley, after referring to the "generally very bad" guesses made by early Christian writers regarding difficult texts, he declares: "I have long thought that the greater part of the book of Daniel is most certainly a very late work of time of the Maccabees; and the pretended prophecy about the Kings of Grecia and Persia, and of the North and South, is mere history, like the poetical prophecies in Vergil and elsewhere. In fact, you can trace distinctly the date when it was written, because the events up to the date are given with historical minuteness, totally unlike the character of real Prophecy; and beyond that date all is imaginary."[131] But for his early death in 1842 Arnold might have

45

advanced Biblical criticism considerably further. For W. R. Greg, writing in 1851, he was, as for other Unitarians, "the most honest theologian of the age".[132]

In 1855 two works appeared both of which owed something to the stimulus of Arnold. The most significant was Benjamin Jowett's *The Epistles of St. Paul to the Thessalonians, Galatians, and Romans, with Critical Notes and Dissertations*, which along with the other volume, viz., A. P. Stanley's *The Epistles of St. Paul to the Corinthians, with Critical Notes and Dissertations*, established a new standard in commentary writing in England. For the *textus receptus* both substituted the new text of Lachmann, and both provided introductions, critical notes, and essays, along with an amended form of the *Authorised Version*. Among the German writings to which Jowett was particularly indebted was F. C. Baur's extremely radical *Paulus, der Apostel Jesu Christi* (1845), which he described as "the ablest book I ever read on St. Paul's Epistles; a remarkable combination of philological and metaphysical power, without the intrusion of Modern Philosophy".[133] This must not be construed to mean, however, that Jowett was in agreement with Baur's fundamental position; and in his discussion of 1 and 2 Thessalonians he goes on to argue against Baur for their authenticity. His own position with regard to the relation of Paul to the Twelve may be described as being in a medial position between the traditional view and that of Baur. Thus he sums up his own position regarding the relation between Paul and the Twelve as: "Independence of each other in their ministry and apostleship; antagonism of the followers, and on one or two occasions of the leaders also; some difference of spirit, together with great personal hostility on the part of the Judaizers to St. Paul, but not of St. Paul to the Twelve."[134] In the appended essays a marked absence of dogmatic prejudice is discernible; indeed, the whole commentary may be said to exemplify Jowett's own *dictum*, promulgated a few years later, viz., that the interpreter's object should be to "interpret the Scripture like any other book".[135] Stanley's volume, though of less critical power and somewhat deficient, furthermore, in scholarly accuracy, was noteworthy for its freedom from the dogmatic exegesis customary at the time, and also for its remarkable power of historical sympathy, which similarly characterized his *Lectures on the History of the Jewish Church*, and which assisted in the development of a realistic approach to Biblical study. His enumeration of the various defects in the *Authorised Version* at the conclusion of the volume[136] may be said to have contributed to the realization of the need for a revision of the *Authorised Version*, which resulted in the *Revised Version* of 1881–5.

Of special importance because of the furore which it aroused and the consequent establishment of the legitimacy of a liberal approach to the Bible in the Anglican Church was Jowett's Essay *On the Interpretation of Scripture* published in 1860 in *Essays and Reviews*. Here Jowett drew attention to the immense variety of interpretation to which the Bible has been subjected in the interest of dogmatic, controversial, and rhetorical considerations. "More than any other subject of human knowledge", he said, "Biblical criticism has hung to the past; it has been hitherto found truer to the traditions of the Church than to the words of Christ."[137] The Bible must be studied not to see what it "may be made to mean, but what it does".[138] He who approaches the Bible in this impartial manner and makes use of the present knowledge "may know more of the original spirit and intention of the authors of the New Testament than all the controversial writers of former ages put together".[139] Jowett spoke boldly of the "way in which the language of Creeds and liturgies" exercises "a disturbing influence on the interpretation of Scripture",[140] and of the "extraordinary and unreasonable importance attached to single words, sometimes of doubtful meaning" in reference to such subjects as "the Personality of the Holy Spirit, Infant Baptism, . . . Original Sin".[141] Naturally the essay received commendation in Unitarian circles. In a leading article the Unitarian periodical, *The Inquirer*, declared: "There is no hope for the orthodox theology in any of its prevailing forms if Mr. Jowett's principles of interpretation are generally accepted. Orthodox critics have a very clear perception of this, and their wrath is proportionably great. From their mouths we may learn that it is not . . . our sectarian partiality alone which discerns in the writings of the Broad Church School the most important confirmation of our most cherished principles,"[142] and Dr. J. R. Beard, founder of the Unitarian College, Manchester, hailed Jowett as "a fellow-believer" and "fellow-inquirer". "The essay", he said, "embodies an undesigned but effectual justification of Unitarianism. Here are the principles of interpretation which are taught to our divinity students while at college; here are the principles of interpretation which underlie the teachings given by our ministers from the pulpit; and here are even results of the same principles of interpretation as set forth in our Unitarian manuals and embodied in our Unitarian sermons. Here they are, those principles and those results, we do not say derived from Unitarian sources, but certainly wonderfully corroborative of our Unitarian position. If these instructions are the independent products of Professor Jowett's own reading and thinking, they are an independent evidence to the truth of Unitarian Christianity."[143]

Two years later J. W. Colenso published "Part One" of his *The Pentateuch and the Book of Joshua Critically Examined*. In it he somewhat unwisely gave expression to some of his conclusions with regard to the authenticity and historicity of the Pentateuch without the critical backing to his opinions which he gave in the subsequent "Parts" of his work, and which might have improved his case in the eyes of many fair-minded readers, for Colenso was soon to be the subject of a heresy trial,[144] which, it may be mentioned, earned him considerable sympathy in Unitarian circles. "The result of my enquiry", Colenso said, "is this, that I have arrived at the conviction,—as painful to myself at first, as it may be to my reader, though painful now no longer under the clear shining Light of Truth,—that the Pentateuch, as a whole, cannot possibly have been written by Moses, or by any one acquainted personally with the facts which it professes to describe, and, further, that the (so-called) Mosaic narrative, by whomsoever written, and though imparting to us, as I fully believe it does, revelations of the Divine Will and Character, cannot be regarded as *historically true*."[145]

Colenso went on to draw attention to the many inconsistencies and contradictory statements—largely of an arithmetical character—to be found in the Pentateuch; and in subsequent "Parts" of his treatise the last of which was published in 1879,he gave the expression to the following critical opinions: that the Pentateuch was composed of three groups of documents, Elohistic, Yahwistic, and Deuteronomistic; that Joshua was a mythical figure; that the Priestly Legislation belongs to the period of the Captivity or later; that Deuteronomy was composed during the reign of either Manasseh or Josiah; and that Chronicles—which do not provide a trustworthy narrative—were to be assigned to a period later by some centuries than the Exile.[146]

Like the contributions in *Essays and Reviews* Colenso's writings were warmly received in Unitarian circles, and Frances P. Cobbe, writing in 1864, declared: "As we said of the Essayists, so must we say of Colenso. If the Church is to be saved it is to be by the honesty of men like these. Few nobler words have been written for many a day than those with which the Bishop expounds the purport of his work and the scope of his ambition."[147]

The foregoing survey, which, though it does not claim to be exhaustive, covers the chief contributions made within the period under consideration, is indicative of the striking similarity of spirit and approach on the part of Unitarians and Broad Churchmen in the matter of Biblical criticism. Though the Unitarians were sometimes inclined to be excessively radical, the same essentially iconoclastic spirit is to be found in some of the more extreme statements of a Jowett or a Colenso, and throughout there is to be seen in the contributions of both Broad Churchmen and Unitarians the same basic appeal to reason, and reverence for truth, however unpalatable, and the same readiness to abandon cherished, but ill-founded, traditions in the light of new discoveries, which gave such offence to the rest of the Churches of their day. Both were pioneers of the critical approach as applied to the Bible, and like all pioneers they made mistakes, but they did not make the mistake of standing still. Writing in 1885 Count Goblet D'Alviella spoke truly, therefore, when he said: "The Unitarians, like the members of the Broad Church party and the liberal Protestants of the Continent, have taken a considerable share in promoting the progress of Biblical criticism."[148]

CHAPTER 3

The Affinity shown in the Attitude towards Biblical Inspiration, Miracles, Everlasting Punishment, the Atonement, and the Divinity of Christ

Higher criticism, the advance of scientific discovery, and reflection on Christian dogma brought about in the nineteenth century much discussion of certain important questions on which—in contrast with the majority in the churches—Unitarians and Broad Churchmen found considerable agreement.

The findings of higher criticism, of course, raised the whole question of the nature of the inspiration of the Bible. If the Biblical records contained historical and literary discrepancies, if in some cases they showed evidence that their authors copied each other, and if they were at variance with scientific knowledge, could they be called inspired? F. W. Robertson was hardly exaggerating when he described "this grand question of Inspiration" as "the deepest question of our day".[1]

Both Unitarians and Broad Churchmen wrote fairly extensively on the subject,[2] and were in agreement that the old theory of verbal inspiration could not stand.

Among the Unitarians, however, there was a tendency to identify the concept of verbal inspiration with inspiration as such, and in rejecting the former to reject the latter also. Thus, for example, Thomas Belsham, on finding that Genesis was made up of various literary strata, and, furthermore, that it expressed views in conflict with science, rejected the inspiration of that book, and made no attempt to formulate an alternative theory of inspiration.[3] Similarly, James Martineau, writing in 1836, took the view that inspiration meant "all the ideas in the minds of certain authors have been rendered infallibly correct",[4] and, on failing to find justification for such a view of the Scriptures, concluded that "we must pronounce them uninspired but truthful, sincere, able, vigorous, but fallible . . .".[5] So too Charles Hennell, in his *Inquiry Concerning the Origin of Christianity*, speaks of "the doctrine of inspiration or of the unquestionable veracity of the Gospel writers",[6] and in his treatment of the Gospels clearly indicates that he rejects such a view of them; and he makes no attempt to produce an alternative theory. Indeed, some Unitarians were positively opposed to the formulation of such theories of inspiration. Thus W. R. Greg, in the *Creed of Christendom* has a chapter entitled "Modern Modifications of the Doctrine of Inspiration" in which he attacks Thomas Arnold's view that inspiration admits of degree and is compatible with error,[7] for, says Greg, "A statement or dogma came from God, or it did not. If it came from God, it must be infallible;—and if it did not, it must be fallible, and may be false."[8] The Coleridgean theory of Biblical inspiration, viz., that "whatever *finds me* bears witness for itself that it has proceeded from a Holy Spirit",[9] also met with Greg's disapproval when the Bible was used as a uniquely authoritative treasury of dogma, for, said Greg: "Of how many hundred books may not the same be said, though in a less degree? In Milton, in Shakespeare, in Plato, in Aeschylus, Mad. (sic) de Stael, aye, even in Byron and Rousseau, who is there that has not found 'words for his inmost thoughts, songs for his joy, utterance for his griefs, and pleadings for his shame'."[10]

Other Unitarian writers, as, for example, Edward Higginson[11] and Charles Beard, while rejecting the inspiration of the Bible, made it plain that they received it as a *record* of inspiration. "We willingly admit", wrote Beard, "the inspiration of those teachers and prophets whose words and acts are recorded in the Bible . . . But it is a very different thing from admitting that the writers of the Biblical books, who are in many cases absolutely unknown to us,—whose names where we possess them, have in many cases more been handed down to us by an uncertain tradition,—were also inspired."[12]

Broad Churchmen, on the other hand, while rejecting the

doctrine of verbal inspiration still retained the concept of inspiration, which they expressed in various ways, some of which were rather vague. Thus Connop Thirlwall, after rejecting the view that "the sacred writers were merely passive organs or instruments of the Holy Spirit",[13] discusses the theories of (a) *suggestion*, according to which there was revealed to the sacred writers that which it is necessary to reveal, and (b) of *superintendence*, according to which the writers were secured "from any material error or mistake".[14] Neither is satisfactory, he says, and concludes that in Biblical inspiration must be seen "the operation of the Spirit, not in any temporary, physical or even intellectual changes wrought in its subjects, but in the continual presence and action of what is vital and essential to Christianity itself".[15] So, too, in a letter quoted by A. P. Stanley in his *Life of Arnold*, the writer says of the latter, "Any accurate, precise, and sharply defined theory of inspiration, to the best of my knowledge, Arnold had not; and, if he had been asked to give one, I think he would have answered that the subject did not admit of one."[16] To such Unitarians as Greg conceptions of inspiration of this kind were dangerous, not so much in themselves, but as being liable to misinterpretation into the popular sense, namely the verbal theory, and made the basis of a dogmatic system, which in his view, they could not sustain. For, according to Greg, only verbal inspiration could have "dogmatic value", i.e., "form the basis of dogmas which are to be received as authoritative, *because* taught in or fairly deduced from the Scriptures".[17]

It has been stated that Unitarians had a tendency to reject the concept of inspiration along with that of the verbal theory, and evidence has been presented in support of that statement. However, even among the writers quoted in that regard, a view of inspiration may be found, which was closely similar to, or identical with, that of certain Broad Church writers—the view, namely, that the Bible, in virtue of its lofty moral and spiritual character, may be said to be "inspired", though differing from other good and holy books not in kind, and only in degree. Thus, while Greg endeavours to show that "the tenet of the Inspiration of the Scriptures is baseless and untenable under any form or modification which leaves to it a dogmatic value",[18] he yet admits to a belief in inspiration in the sense of "that elevation of all the spiritual faculties by the action of God upon the heart, which is shared by all devout minds, though in different degrees, and which is consistent with infinite error".[19] So, when Thomas Arnold remarks that "the difference between the inspiration of the common and perhaps unworthy Christian who merely said that 'Jesus was the Lord', and that of Moses or St. Paul, or St. John, is almost to our eyes beyond measuring",[20] and yet continues, "Still the position remains, that the highest degree of inspiration given to man has still suffered to exist along with it a portion of human fallibility and corruption,"[21] Greg comments: "If Dr. Arnold chooses to assume, as he appears to do, that every man who acknowledges Jesus to be the Christ, is inspired, after a fashion, and means, . . . simply to affirm that Paul and John were inspired, just as all good and great minds are inspired, only in a superior degree, proportioned to their superior greatness and goodness—then, neither we, nor anyone, will think it worth while to differ with him."[22] Similar was Martineau's conception, expressed in 1841, of "the strictly Divine and Inspired Character of our own highest Desires and Affections",[23] or when in his last book, after referring to the "common presence of God in the conscience of mankind",[24] he declared: "Were not our humanity itself an Emmanuel, there could be no Christ to bear the name."[25] So, too, J. J. Tayler speaks of "my distinct ascription of all true religion to the inspiration of God as its original source. My whole religious philosophy rests on this fundamental principle, which I hold with deep and daily strengthening conviction. In fact, I have not a less, but a greater faith in Divine Revelation than other Christians. I cannot resist the belief that the particles of a divine life which preserved from absolute moral rottenness even the crude, dark masses of heathen superstition, came ultimately from the Supreme Fountain of light, and that the constant, ever active presence of God's Spirit underlies every genuine and earnest manifestation of our religious nature",[26]

For these Unitarians all religions, and all religious books, were "inspired", insofar as they expressed moral and spiritual truth, and "the difference between them was not one of kind, but of degree".[27]

How closely many Broad Churchmen approximated to the same position may be seen from the following extracts from Broad Church writers. "Martineau's views about Inspiration I think, on the whole, correct,"[28] wrote F. W. Robertson, and he added later, "the prophetic power, in which I suppose is chiefly exhibited that which we mean by inspiration, depends almost entirely on moral greatness. The prophet discerned large principles true for all time—principles social, political, ecclesiastical and principles of life—chiefly by largeness of heart and sympathy of spirit with God's spirit. This is my conception of inspiration".[29] Rowland Williams, in *Essays and Reviews*, spoke of religious, moral, critical, and scientific considerations which had "widened the idea of Revelation for the old world, and deepened it for ourselves; not removing the footsteps of the Eternal from Palestine, but tracing them on other shores".[30] "The moral constituents of our nature", he said, "so often contrasted with Revelation, should rather be considered parts of its instrumentality";[31] and, later, in reference to the "Eternal Spirit; that abiding influence, which . . . underlies all others",[32] he more specifically declared: "If such a Spirit did not dwell in the Church, the Bible would not be inspired, for the Bible is before all things, the written voice of the congregation. Bold as such a theory of inspiration may sound . . . it is the only one to which the facts of Scripture answer. The sacred writers acknowledge themselves men of like passions with ourselves, and we are promised illumination from the spirit which dwelt in them. Hence, when we find . . . the idea of the Church being an inspired society, instead of objecting that every one of us is fallible, we should define inspiration consistently with the facts of Scripture and of human nature. These would neither exclude the idea of fallibility among Israelites of old, nor teach us to quench the Spirit in true hearts for ever."[33] Three years later, it is interesting to observe, the Unitarian scholar, J. J. Tayler, wrote the following passage, in which it is perhaps not illegitimate to see a reflection of the previously quoted passage from the Broad Churchman: "In what relation do we perceive Church and Scripture to stand towards each other now? Neither of them can claim to be primal authorities. Both are derivative and secondary. Both of them are products of one and the same Spirit. The Spirit created the church before it created Scripture and gradually drew out Scripture from the bosom of the Church as an expression of its deepest thought and living consciousness. Neither Scripture nor the Church would be anything more to us than mere historical phenomena, without the unbroken continuity of the Spirit in the hearts of believers."[34] Benjamin Jowett expressed his "last words on inspiration" in a private memorandum as follows:

"1. Were the writers of the New Testament inspired when they wrote in any other sense than they were during the rest of their lives?

2. Is there any essential difference between the apostles St. Paul and St. Bernard, and if so, how is this difference to be defined or ascertained?

3. Is there any difference between St. Bernard and Plato except that they were men of genius of a different kind—the one a religious genius, the other a philosophical and poetical genius?

4. But if so, inspiration must be extended to all men who rise above themselves, who get out of themselves, who have anticipations of truths which they cannot realize; who live not in the present and individual, but in the future and universal world.

5. But if so, every great and good man is inspired, or none are inspired, and all the great thoughts of mankind are to be treated as part of the sacred inheritance."[35]

So, too, finally, H. R. Haweis declared in 1885, "If by inspiration you mean a level of moral teaching and spiritual truth above the average of each age, then the Bible is inspired, for it records the highest levels of moral thought and religious feeling reached by successive ages, as well as the exceptional level reached by specially gifted persons called prophets and seers."[36]

If higher criticism raised the question of Inspiration, it also raised, as did scientific discovery, the further question of miracles. Did they really happen? On this issue, again, Unitarians and Broad Churchmen found a considerable measure of agreement.

At the beginning of the century Unitarians accepted the traditional belief in miracles, the latter being received as an important authentication of the teaching of Jesus. Later, under the influence of Biblical criticism and the knowledge of scientific discoveries, belief in miracles weakened among them, and in spite of some opposition from the less important Biblically-based wing of Unitarianism, finally disappeared by the end of the century.

As early as 1836 James Martineau could refer, in his *Rationale*, to "partial misconceptions of fact"[37] and "evident misrepresentations of miracles"[38] in the New Testament, opposing, moreover, the view "that no attempts should be made to explain the alleged supernatural events of scripture by the operation of natural causes"[39] for the latter was a necessary critical procedure. But he yet believed in miracles, and added later: "should these attempts to reduce the facts of the evangelical history to common events be successful, the Gospel falls: nor is there any intelligible sense in which one, who thinks that the preternatural may be thus banished from the birth and infancy of our faith, can continue to take the name of Christian".[40] Martineau, however, had meanwhile established a friendship with the former Noetic scholar, Joseph Blanco White, who had by now openly acknowledged his Unitarianism, and who vigorously opposed what he called "the dangerous mistake of supposing the essence of Christianity to be inseparable from the firm belief in historical miracles", which, "the growth of the human mind . . . will every day more and more oppose".[41] In a long letter written in 1836, Blanco White urged upon Martineau the considerable uncertainty in which historical miracles stood. "I cannot conceive", he wrote, "how any unprejudiced person to whom the difficulties of historical proof are known, can deliberately assert, that the great mass of mankind of all countries and ages can receive Christianity upon historical grounds; especially, if upon such grounds it be their duty to believe in the miracles both of the Old and the New Testament".[42] Blanco White's argument was not without effect, and by 1840 Martineau's correspondence reveals that he had come round to the same viewpoint.[43] But it was not until 1845, in the preface to the third edition of his *Rationale*, that Martineau announced his distinction between "*philosophical anti-supernaturalism*, which regards miracles as *per se* incredible, and disowns whatever is irreducible to necessary causation, and *historical anti-supernaturalism*, which, from a critical estimate of testimony, questions certain particular miracles, without any abatement of the preternatural claims of the religion in whose records they appear".[44] The former was "essentially irreligious", but the latter need not affect a man's religious classification as a Christian, for "the state of mind . . . which recognizes what is beyond nature in Christ, and owns a divine and 'supernatural' authority in his religion, may co-exist with doubt, or even disbelief in the miracles recorded in the Scriptures".[45]

Many years later in his *Seat of Authority in Religion* (1890) Martineau laid it down as a critical rule that "miraculous events cannot be regarded as adequately attested, in presence of natural causes accounting for belief in their occurrence";[46] and though he declared that "our stock of known laws" does not exclude "an anomalous phenomenon as impossible and entitle us to say 'It did not happen' ", he virtually committed himself to a total disbelief in miracles when he added, "It does authorize us to say . . . 'Granting its occurrence, you can never tell that it was a miracle'; for there is always room for the unexpected in the gaps of undetermined law; and when assigned to its place there, it belongs to the sphere of Nature, and not to what is beyond nature, as you want your miracle to be."[47] Nevertheless he still maintained that want of adequate evidence alone should be the ground for questioning the historical validity of miracles reported in the Gospels.[48]

In the same year that Martineau wrote the preface to his third edition of the *Rationale*, J. J. Tayler similarly maintained that Christianity consisted in "deep sympathy with the spirit of Christ", and rejected in this connection the indispensability of belief in miracles, citing Blanco White as an example of "those devout persons who, unable to assure themselves of the reality of these facts, still acknowledge with their hearts what they feel to be divine in Christ's doctrine and person".[49]

Meanwhile, in 1838, C. C. Hennell had devoted four chapters of his *Inquiry*, besides a chapter on the Resurrection and Ascension, to a discussion of miracles. His approach may be seen from the following quotation: "In common life marvellous tales are often met with, which, on taking the trouble to trace them back through various stages to their source, we find to have originated in something perfectly intelligible and natural. And when we have done this in some instances, we conclude that the same result would follow in the case of similar tales, coming to us through the same channels, although in the latter case we might not have the means of following up such a tedious investigation."[50] Again and again, and often with considerable cogency, Hennell found a naturalistic interpretation for the miracles he discussed, and his verdict regarding the resurrection was that "upon the whole the accounts of the appearance of Jesus after his death are incredible".[51] For him, like the previously mentioned writers, belief in miracles was not an essential part of Christianity. "Although", he said, "the belief in the miraculous origin of Christianity forms at present a prominent feature in the creeds of all sects of progressive Christians, it would be an unnecessary and perhaps injudicious limitation to hold the relinquishment of this belief is equivalent to an entire renunciation of the Christian religion."[52]

The same point was made in 1851 when W. R. Greg urged that "miracles are not the real basis of Christianity, and cannot be a safe foundation on which to rest its claims, inasmuch as miracles can never be proved by *documentary* evidence—least of all by such documentary evidence as we possess".[53] There was a serious lack of personal and concurrent testimony in the narratives concerned; and, for Greg, the miracles were "probably either remarkable occurrences elevated into supernatural ones by the general supernaturalistic tendencies of the age, or examples of wonderful healing powers, the original accounts of which have become strangely inter-mingled and overlaid with fiction in the process of transmission".[54]

In the mid-nineteenth century, however, not all Unitarians were prepared to relinquish their belief in miracles so readily. The influence of the older, Biblically-based wing of Unitarianism, which stressed the evidential value of miracles, was still felt; and in 1853 Edward Higginson wrote: "I accept . . . fully and frankly, the miraculous in Christianity as its very basis."[55] But it is interesting to observe that Higginson went on to draw a distinction between "physical" or "outward" and "spiritual" or "inward"[56] miracles, which considerably weakened the force of his previous statement. In the time of Jesus it was the physical miracles which had the greatest evidential value; but, thought Higginson, it was the spiritual miracles, namely, "the character of Jesus, the heavenly wisdom of his precepts, the purity and elevation of his morality, the breadth of his philanthropy",[57] etc., which had the evidential value in the nineteenth century. "It would be a great mistake", he admitted, "to attempt to prove the truth of Christianity to an inquirer *now*, by appealing first to the outward miracles of Christ. Those miracles are the very things that *now* chiefly require proving. We do not believe Christianity to be divine because of its outward miracles; but we accept its outward miracles as belonging to it . . . when we believe it to be divine in itself."[58]

As the century wore on the importance of belief in miracles, however, continued to decline. No longer could they be held to be essential; and it must not be thought that the expression of this viewpoint was confined to serious books read only by the few. The Unitarian weekly newspapers also took their share. Thus *The Unitarian Herald*, which circulated widely among the industrial congregations of Lancashire and Yorkshire[59] declared in 1863: "We do not consider one of the *essential* doctrines of Unitarianism to be belief in the Gospel miracles. We think this may be left an open question, among those who agree in the worship of God our Father as disciples of Christ."[60] And in the following year *The Inquirer*, which had a much wider circulation, declared: "If a man can be a Christian after disbelieving the Deity of Christ, and the popular interpretation of the Atonement, surely a disbelief in miracles cannot unchristianise him."[61]

At the close of the century, in a volume to which several leading Unitarians were contributors, Walter Lloyd, after a discussion of some of the more important Biblical miracles, stated: "This brief survey of the narratives of the principal miracles to be found in the Old and New Testaments justifies us in the conclusion that they are not founded upon facts, but arose out of a mental condition, a mixture of piety and credulity, which is a common psychological phenomenon which has been as common in the Christian Church as elsewhere";[62] and he added later: "The real greatness of Jesus did not consist in his alleged ability to perform miracles, but in the marvellous spiritual influence he has exercised over the human race."[63]

Broad Churchmen exhibited a similar approach to miracles. As early as 1829 H. H. Milman displayed, as has been seen in the preceding chapter, a disposition to account for miracles in naturalistic terms; and in 1852 F. W. Robertson roundly declared: "I hold that the attempt to rest Christianity on miracles . . . is essentially the vilest rationalism."[64] But, for the most part, explicit statements on the miracle question by Broad Churchmen came rather later in the century.

The first noteworthy Broad Church contribution to the subject came in 1860 when, in *Essays and Reviews*, Baden Powell declared that "if miracles were in the estimation of a former age among the chief *supports* of Christianity, they are at present among the main *difficulties*, and hindrances to its acceptance".[65]

His approach was essentially that of the scientist committed to the principle of the uniformity of nature.[66] Exceptions to known laws were brought under larger laws. Testimony might be given to the occurrence of an unusual phenomenon, but "no amount of attestation of innumerable and honest witnesses, would ever convince anyone versed in mathematical or mechanical science, that a person had squared a circle or discovered perpetual motion".[67] Testimony, in fact, was not the vital issue. "The essential question of miracles", he said, "stands quite apart from any question of *testimony*. . . . It is not the *mere fact*, but the *cause* or *explanation* of it, which is the point at issue."[68] And Baden Powell's conclusion on the question of miracles was as follows: "An alleged miracle can be regarded in one of two ways;—either (1) abstractedly as a physical event, and therefore to be investigated by reason and physical evidence, and referred to physical causes, possibly to *known* causes, but at all events to some higher cause or law, if at present unknown; it then ceases to be supernatural, yet still might be appealed to in support of religious truth, especially as referring to the state of knowledge and apprehensions of the parties addressed in past ages; or (2) as connected with religious doctrine, regarded in a sacred light, asserted on the authority of inspiration. In this case it ceases to be capable of investigation by reason, or to own its dominion; it is accepted on religious grounds, and can appeal only to the principle and influence of faith."[69] That Baden Powell's sympathy was with the first alternative there can be no question. Christianity did not depend upon external signs; it was its own evidence; and, like the previously quoted Unitarians, he declared: "The more knowledge advances, the more it has been, and will be, acknowledged that Christianity as a real religion, must be viewed apart from connexion with physical things."[70]

Benjamin Jowett, writing in a private journal during the period 1873–6, declared: "Whether we like to admit it or not, the belief in miracles is fading away, and can only be maintained by a violent effort, which must revive many other superstitions";[71] and in 1886 he wrote: "The conception of miracles may become impossible and absurd."[72] There could be no "return to the belief in facts which are disproved, e.g. miracles, the narratives of creation, of Mount Sinai".[73] According to A. H. Craufurd, "the Master of Balliol seemed to look upon disbelief in miracles as the one sign of religious enlightenment".[74]

Meanwhile, the Broad Church layman, Matthew Arnold, had declared that "the objections to miracles do, and more and more will, without insistence, without attack, without controversy, make their own force felt; and that the sanction of

Christianity, if Christianity is not to be lost along with miracles, must be found elsewhere";[75] and in 1883 he made the categorical statement: "Miracles do not happen."[76]

Three years later, in *The Kernel and the Husk*—a book, incidentally, which was warmly received in Unitarian circles[77]— E. A. Abbott declared: "There may come—I think there will soon come—a time when belief in miracles will be found so incompatible with the reverence which we ought to feel for the Supreme Order as almost to necessitate superstition, and to encourage immorality in the holder of the belief: and then it might be necessary to express one's condemnation of miracles plainly and even aggressively."[78] His approach was similar to that expressed in the first quotation from Hennell.[79] Thus, in reference to his rejection of miracles, he wrote: "It is not simply because there is not sufficient evidence for them; it is in great measure because there is evidence against them. For when you can show how a supposed miracle may naturally have occurred, and how the miraculous account may naturally and easily have sprung up, I think that amounts to evidence against the miracle. And of course when you find yourself compelled to explain in this way a large number of miracles in the Old Testament, it becomes more probable than before that the rest are susceptible of some natural explanation."[80] And when, later, Abbott says that "the criticism of the New Testament, and the researches of science, and the closer study of the life of Christ Himself, all converge on this conclusion—that Christ conquered the world, not by working miracles, but by living such a life and dying such a death as might be lived and died by the Son of God, incarnate as Son of man, and self-subjected to all the physical limitations of humanity; and by bequeathing to mankind, after His death, such a Spirit as was correspondent to His own nature"[81] he was expressing essentially the same thought as that contained in the final statement quoted earlier from Walter Lloyd.[82]

The foregoing questions were raised by the results of higher criticism and scientific discovery. Other important questions were raised by reflection on Christian doctrine.

During the nineteenth century the majority of Christians, whether belonging to the Anglican Church or the ranks of Nonconformity, believed in the doctrine of everlasting punishment; and the appeal of much Evangelical preaching was set against the background of the threat of everlasting punishment. In protest against the rejection of this doctrine in *Essays and Reviews* eleven thousand clergymen of the Church of England signed a Declaration in 1864 asserting their "firm belief" that "the 'punishment' of the 'cursed' equally with the 'life' of the 'righteous' is 'everlasting' ", and this "without reserve or qualification".[83]

Unitarians, by contrast, rejected the doctrine, and this rejection was a natural corollary of their repudiation of the doctrine of original sin and their warm espousal of the doctrine of the Fatherhood of God. Thus Lant Carpenter, writing in 1820, stated in reference to belief in everlasting punishment: "In rejecting this opinion (which has made more unbelievers in Christianity than any other cause except the vices of professed Christians) Unitarians are universally agreed; and the connection is close, and I think, indissoluble, between the fundamental doctrines of Unitarianism and the divine character and dispensation which forbids us to make his glory depend on something different from, and even opposed to, his justice and his goodness. I should be disposed to go further, and say that those views of the divine character, to which I refer, inevitably lead to the belief, that there will be a time when all the rational creatures of God will have been purified from every pollution, and made fit for holiness."[84] Unitarians, however, did not wish to inculcate a careless attitude; and, in a manner reminiscent of that of the Broad Churchmen when dealing with a difficult doctrine whose essential truth, while discarding the husk, they wished to preserve, W. R. Greg, writing in 1851, declared: "The doctrine of the eternity of future punishments, false as it must be in its ordinary signification, contains a glimpse of one of the most awful and indisputable truths ever presented to human understanding—viz., the eternal and ineffaceable consequences of our every action, the fact that every word and deed produces effects which must, by the very nature of things reverberate through all time, so that the whole futurity would be different had that word never been spoken, or that deed enacted."[85] Similarly, a writer in the *Prospective Review* asserted three years later: "Hell is a diseased condition of the soul, its indwelling wretchedness and retribution, wherever it may be, as when the light of day tortures a sick eye. Heaven is a right healthy condition of the soul, its indwelling integrity and concord in whatever realms it may reside, as when the sunshine bathes the healthy orb of vision with entrancing delight";[86] and he added subsequently: "We have no reason to suppose that probation closes with the closing of the present life, but every relevant consideration leads us to conclude that the same great constitution of laws pervades all worlds and reigns throughout eternity, so that the fate of souls is not unchangeably fixed at death. No analogy indicates that after death all will be thoroughly different from what it is before death. Rather do all analogies argue that the hell and heaven of the future will be the aggravation, or mitigation, or continuation of the perdition and salvation of the present."[87]

If the foregoing seems to be a rather austere doctrine, it must be remembered that it is infinitely more attractive than the then prevailing doctrine of everlasting punishment. For while maintaining a responsible attitude to sin, Unitarians yet took the view that punishment was remedial. Thus the American Unitarian James Freeman Clarke, whose writings were popular among English Unitarians and certainly represented their point of view, stated in 1884: "Unitarians oppose the common doctrine of everlasting punishment as being hostile to the sovereignity, wisdom, justice, and mercy of the Divine Being, and also as limiting the redeeming power of Christ and his Gospel. They believe that, the object of punishment being reformatory, it will only continue until the sinner shall be reformed. . . . Unitarians believe in many hells and many heavens, according to the character and condition of each person."[88] The Unitarian doctrine, in fact, was a message of hope and consolation; and many, hitherto either plagued or affronted by the "belief which has produced more insanity and atheism than any other cause connected with religion",[89] were glad to listen to such a preacher as Crosskey who, in 1888, expressed the Unitarian position in the following dramatic way: "If ye then being evil know how to give good gifts to your children, how much more shall your Father which is in heaven give good things to them that ask him? This principle makes short work of many a fierce dogma. Would a father torment a child for ever? Impossible; must be the reply. Then we conclude at once that the doctrine of 'Eternal Punishment' must be false."[90]

The Broad Churchmen were also unhappy about this doctrine, and when they did not maintain a diplomatic silence on the subject, were critical of the doctrine in question.[91] The first noteworthy attack came in 1853 when F. D. Maurice stated in his *Theological Essays* that "Eternity", whether in reference to life or punishment, "has nothing to do with time or duration".[92] Perdition, in his view, was loss of the knowledge of God and Christ, which it is life to know. "I dare not pronounce . . . what are the possibilities", he said, "of resistance in a human will to the loving will of God. There are times when they seem to me— thinking of myself more than of others—almost infinite. I am obliged to believe in an abyss of love which is deeper than the abyss of death: I dare not lose faith in that love. I sink into death, eternal death if I do. I must feel that this love is encompassing the universe. More about it I cannot know, but God knows. I leave myself and all to Him."[93] Because his statements seemed to Principal Jelf "to throw an atmosphere of doubt on the simple meaning of the word *eternal* and to convey a general notion of ultimate salvation to all"[94] Maurice was dismissed from his position as Professor of Theology at King's College, London.

More serious consequences resulted for H. B. Wilson, when, seven years later in *Essays and Reviews* he gave expression to hope of an intermediate state after death and the ultimate escape of all from divine condemnation. "If we look abroad in the world", he said in the concluding paragraph of his essay, "and regard the neutral character of the multitude, we are at a loss to apply to them, either the promises, or the denunciations of revelation."[95] This spectacle demanded, he thought, that "we must . . . entertain a hope that there shall be found, after the great adjudication, receptacles suitable for those who shall be infants, not as to years of terrestial life, but as to spiritual development—nurseries as it were and seed grounds, where the undeveloped may grow up under new conditions—the stunted may become strong, and the perverted restored"; and he looked forward to the time when "all, both small and great, shall find a refuge in the bosom of the Universal Parent, to repose, or be quickened into higher life, in ages to come, according to His Will".[96] For the expression of this view—which is remarkably similar to that expressed at the conclusion of the previously quoted passage from Freeman Clarke—Wilson was prosecuted for heresy and sentenced by the Court of Arches in 1861 to suspension *ab officio et beneficio* for a year; and although the verdict was reversed by the Judicial Committee of the Privy Council in February 1864, *Essays and Reviews* was synodically condemned by the Convocation of the province of Canterbury only a few months later. It was the decision of the Privy Council, however, that was legally binding, and Dean Stanley wrote: "That the Church of England does not hold . . . Eternity of Torment, is now, I trust, fixed for ever. I hope that all will now go on smoothly, and that the Bible may be really read without those terrible nightmares. Thank God!"[97]

In 1861 J. W. Colenso published his *Commentary on the Epistle to the Romans*, which is chiefly significant for its challenge to traditional doctrines. "I now declare", he wrote, "that I can no longer maintain . . . the doctrine of the endlessness of 'future punishments',—that I dare not dogmatise at all on the matter—that I can only . . . leave it in the hands of the righteous and merciful Judge."[98] Like F. D. Maurice he saw that "the word 'eternal' does not mean 'endless' ",[99] and like the Unitarian writers previously quoted declared: "When we consider a multitude of cases, it is inconceivable that the hour of death should, under the Government of a Just and Holy Judge, draw a line sharply between all those who shall be admitted to endless blessedness, and all those who shall be consigned to endless woe. The infinite shades of difference, which discriminate the moral characters of men, can, indeed, and will be taken into account by Him who knows the hearts and lives of all."[100] But no Unitarian could have been more forthright than when Colenso boldly declared in reference to the doctrine of everlasting punishment: "Our hearts . . . revolt at such a dogma, as a blasphemy upon the Name and Character of the High and Holy One, and refuse to believe it, though a thousand texts of Scripture should be produced, which may seem, at first sight, to assert it."[101]

It was about this time that Charles Voysey preached the sermon against everlasting punishment which earned for him his dismissal from the curacy of a London parish. Though Voysey claimed that the "incumbent admitted that he substantially agreed"[103] with the sermon, he had evidently ignored Jowett's personal advice to him to observe that it was "impossible for a clergyman holding liberal opinions to be too cautious in the mode of stating them".[104] How cautious Jowett could be when dealing with the doctrine in question may be gathered from the following extract from one of his sermons: "Is the justice of God reconcilable with the everlasting damnation of a portion of his creatures? My brethren, I am not concerned to answer such objections. There is nothing wrong in such feelings, so far as they express not any laxity about sin and evil, but a jealous desire to vindicate above all things the justice of God. . . . Let us not speak of an infinite punishment for a finite sin. Neither on the other hand, let us assume that a time will come when every man will be restored to the grace and favour of God. . . . But let us rather say that God 'will reward every man according to his works' and that the punishment of mankind in another world will be perfectly just because afflicted by God; the least evil that we do shall not be without consequences, the least good not wholly unrewarded."[105] Voysey's indiscretions, however, increased, and in 1871 he was finally deprived of his benefice as Rector of Healaugh, for denying, among other things, the deity of Christ. In his subsequent career he had fully justified the argument of the bishop who told him: "If you take away the doctrine of endless punishment, you take away all need of an atonement, you take away all need of a Divine Saviour, and the very Deity of our Lord becomes imperilled."[106]

The abandonment of the doctrine of everlasting punishment was, in fact, quite frequently one of the preliminary steps in many cases towards the adoption of a Broad Church or Unitarian position. It was, for example, one of the first doctrines to be given up by Stopford Brooke in his passage from an Evangelical to a Broad Church point of view;[107] and when many years later, in 1878, he impatiently declared of the doctrine: "It ought not now to be a matter of discussion at all. That intolerable doctrine ought to be clean swept out of the English Church. Not only would religion be the better for its destruction, but society, and Government, and literature and art."[108] Only two years were to elapse before he left the Church of England to become a Unitarian.

After quoting Tennyson's remark made in 1869 that "the general English view of God is as of an immeasurable clergyman; and some mistake the devil for God"[109] Elliott-Binns observed: "That this view has largely passed away, though not, unfortunately, entirely, was in the main due to the work of the Broad Churchmen. In particular they succeeded in modifying two doctrines in a more Christian direction—those concerning the Future Punishment of the wicked, and the Atonement"[110]— and his statement is broadly true, though it does less than justice to the steady and persistent influence of Unitarian writers and preachers in the same great cause.

If the Unitarians and Broad Churchmen adopted a similar attitude with regard to the doctrine of everlasting punishment, it was natural enough that there should be an extension of this viewpoint to another doctrine of major importance in the nineteenth century—the doctrine of the Atonement in its then traditional form as a vicarious sacrifice.

The nineteenth-century Unitarian attitude to the substitutionary theory was, of course, a continuation and development of the work begun in an earlier age by Socinus.[111] It was an attitude at once rationalistic and profoundly religious, for it was based upon a keen awareness of the goodness of God. Thus John Kenrick, writing of the traditional theory in 1817, could say: "With all its cumbrous apparatus, does it make one truth respecting the nature of God, or the duty of man, more clear or more impressive, than the simple statement that God forgives their sins to those who forsake them, and sent Christ into the world to teach and die, that he might thus reclaim them from those sins, by an example which his death must crown and doctrine which his death must seal?";[122] and summing up the Unitarian objections to the substitutionary theory more than thirty years later John Wright declared: "The doctrine of the Atonement is untrue, because (1) it contradicts the justice and love of God; (2) it is inconsistent with all our notions of the nature and purpose of punishment; (3) it has practically a tendency to discourage moral effort, by leading men to suppose they may sin and not suffer for it."[113]

Unitarians were not unmindful that much of the language of Scripture regarding the death of Christ was of a sacrificial character. But this was explained as being figurative and the result of the nature of the thought-forms of the time in which Jesus lived. Thus Bache declared in 1854: "Is there, then, no sacrificial efficacy . . . to be ascribed to the death of Christ? *None whatever in fact*, I answer distinctly. None whatever in fact, though *some* efficacy, and that of great importance, too, in *figure*."[114] "The early Christian writers who were converts from Judaism", said Wright, "naturally compared the death of Christ to the sacrifices to which, in their former religion, they had been accustomed. Such language as applied to Christ is, however, entirely *figurative*, and is no more to be literally understood than it is to be taken as a sanction of the Hebrew practice of slaughtering animals on the altar."[115] And though Unitarians might point out that ὑπέρ meant "for the sake of" and not "instead of" as was demanded by the doctrine of substitution,[116] it was yet felt that there was danger in "urging too closely the import of any language, which in a figurative sense may be highly descriptive and appropriate, but which in a literal sense would be untenable itself, or contradictory of other figurative expressions interpreted with the same indiscreet literalness".[117]

Unitarians were insistent that the Atonement consisted in the reconciliation of man to God, and not of God to man; and their theory of Christ's function in this was exemplarist. Thus David Maginnis declared in 1859: "Point to him who was the great Captain of our salvation on the field of duty—the well-beloved of the Father; point to him, not as a God enacting a part (in which case or any allied thereto, his example loses its power), but, as the Gospel represents him, 'the Son of Man' 'made perfect through sufferings'—'in all points tempted like as we are, yet without sin'; do this, and men are encouraged, their hearts are strengthened, their hopes brightened, and their hands nerved for any struggle duty may require,—feeling assured that under God they can do all things, inspired and strengthened by the example of Christ."[118] Similarly James Martineau, though strenuously opposing the "heathenish" substitutionary theory, averred: "A Mediator may do much indeed to reconcile my alienated mind to God. He may personally rise before me with a purity and greatness so unique as to give me faith in diviner things than I had known before, and by his higher image turn my eye towards the Highest of all";[119] and summarizing Unitarian belief *The Inquirer* stated in 1886 that Unitarians "deny the commonly received doctrine of atonement, but affirm the reconciliation of man to God through the life and work of Christ".[120]

Among the Broad Churchmen, there was a similar dislike of the substitutionary or transactional conception of the Atonement. According to this theory, F. W. Robertson stated in a sermon preached in 1849, the Atonement "has been represented as if the majesty of Law demanded a victim: and so as it glutted its insatiate thirst, one victim would do as well as another—the surer and the more innocent the better. It has been exhibited as if Eternal love resolved in fury to strike, and so as He had His blow, it mattered not whether it fell on the whole world or on the precious head of His own chosen Son";[121] and he added:

"from a view so horrible, no wonder if Unitarianism has recoiled".[122] As to his own view of the Atonement his second biographer, Frederick Arnold, declared of Robertson: "His idea of atonement is that Christ saves simply by realizing in His own Person the ideal humanity—and by the constraining influence of His love upon the heart."[123] How similar to those of Unitarians Robertson's views of the nature of salvation could be, may be gathered from the following extract on the subject of the sacrifice of Christ: "Does the sacrifice save me from that which is worse than all pain, the feeling of God's wrath, the sense of banishment from the presence of His beauty and His love? The reply to that is, It does. Realise the spirit of the Cross —the surrender of self-will in love—feel, that is, believe, that God is love. . . . Only the appropriation of the Spirit of the Cross redeems. Love transmutes all. . . . Salvation is goodness, humbleness, love,"[124] which expresses essentially the same view as that in the following passage from J. J. Tayler, the distinguished Unitarian theologian, who urged that the Christian mind should "look for salvation in the *spirit* of Christ himself, wrought in the believing soul, and becoming the inward principle of a higher moral life".[125] "This spirit of Christ", he continued, "involves three elements: subjection of will and endeavour to the will of the everlasting Father; affectionate sympathy with humanity in all its stages of development; and the sure expectation of a more glorious futurity both for the individual and for the species. All these elements are expressed and embodied, with a surpassing beauty and power, in the life of Christ: and to sympathise with that life, to baptise our hearts into its redundant spirit of faith and love, to look up to Christ as our spiritual helper and guide to a higher world,—is belief unto salvation, an entrance into the kingdom of God."[126]

The substitutionary theory found another opponent in F. D. Maurice. The crude transactional assumption upon which it was based "was horrible to Maurice",[127] and in his *Theological Essays* he denounced the view that "an innocent person can save the guilty from the consequences of his guilt by taking these upon himself".[128] But Maurice's viewpoint is perhaps best expressed in the following extract from a sermon on the doctrine of sacrifice. "The theory of a propitiation", he said, "not set forth by God, but devised to influence His mind— of a propitiation that does not declare God's righteousness *in* the forgiveness of sins, but which makes it possible for Him to forgive sins *though* He is righteous—this scheme changes all the relations of the Creator and creature; this scheme does build up a priestcraft which subverts utterly the morality of the Bible, because it subverts its theology."[129] How significant Maurice's opposition was may be gathered from the following observation made by F. J. Powicke, writing in 1930: "Sermons on the Atonement were common enough 50 or 60 years ago. They are not so common now, and may it be said that they are not so common now because 50 or 60 years ago they were concerned with transactional theories of the Atonement, and because Maurice did much to sweep all these away?"[130]

But in Benjamin Jowett the substitutionary theory met a perhaps even more formidable adversary. In the essay on the Atonement appended to the first edition of his *Epistles of St. Paul to the Thessalonians, Galatians and Romans* he attacked the current understanding of the doctrine with passionate vehemence; and, when four years later the second edition was published in 1859, with a revised and fuller statement of his position, his indignation was unabated. "The doctrine of the Atonement", he said, "has often been explained in a way at which our moral feelings revolt."[131]

After setting forth the traditional understanding of the doctrine, with its ideas of the appeasement of the Divine wrath by the sacrifice of Christ, and imputed sin and imputed righteousness, he went on to maintain "1. that these conceptions of the work of Christ have no foundation in Scripture; 2. that their growth may be traced in ecclesiastical history; 3. that the only sacrifice, atonement, or satisfaction with which the Christian has to do, is a moral and spiritual one; not the pouring out of blood upon the earth, but the living sacrifice 'to do thy will, O God'; in which the believer has part as well as his Lord".[132]

Like the Unitarians he drew attention to the figurative

character of the sacrificial language and "the inconsistency of the figures".[133] Such language is "a figure of speech borrowed from the Old Testament" and is "not to be explained by the analogy of the Levitical sacrifices".[134] It is "only a mode of speaking common at a time when the rites and ceremonies of the Jewish law were passing away and beginning to receive a spiritual meaning".[135] "Our Lord", he said, "never describes His own work in the language of atonement or sacrifice," and thus Jowett concluded that "nothing is signified by this language, or at least nothing essential, beyond what is implied in the teaching of our Lord himself".[136] And believing that the language of atonement and sacrifice "is not the expression of any objective relation in which the work of Christ stands to His Father",[137] he declared in the concluding paragraph of his essay: "If our Saviour were to come again to earth, which of all the theories of atonement and sacrifice would he sanction with his authority? Perhaps none of them, yet perhaps all may be consistent with a true service of Him. The question has no answer."[138]

J. W. Colenso was another doughty opponent of the substitutionary theory to give expression to his views on the subject in a commentary. In his *Commentary on the Epistle to the Romans* he boldly declared: "Once for all let it be stated distinctly, there is not a single passage in the whole of the New Testament, which supports the dogma of modern theology that our Lord died for our sins, in the sense of dying *instead of* us, dying *in our place*, or dying so as to bear the punishment or penalty of our sins";[139] and, like the Unitarians, he pointed out that "the Greek preposition . . . rendered by 'for', *never*, in any single instance, means 'in our stead', but 'on our behalf' ".[140]

But the expression of the Broad Church position was not confined to scholarly exposition, and it was in a much more popular style that H. R. Haweis wrote in 1885: "When a seaman swims to shore and expires from exhaustion, bearing his precious freight of a human life, it may be some weak and fainting woman or child saved by his exertions, he hopes and prays to get to land alive himself. His death is a sublime accident. So

74

Christ would fain have done his work without the shedding of blood."[141]

The result of all this was that, as A. M. Ramsey has said, "many Broad Churchmen tended to embrace a purely 'exemplarist' doctrine";[142] and Canon W. H. Fremantle might have been a Unitarian when he defined the Atonement as "a reconciliation of the heart and will to God by the moral power of the Cross".[143] But there was also a further result, and that of greater importance for this study of Unitarian and Broad Church relations. In the substitutionary scheme of the Atonement the divinity of Christ is essential, nothing less than a divine substitute being required to bear the punishment for the world's sin. But, as Hector Macpherson has remarked: "In the Broad Church scheme the uniqueness of Christ and His mission is considerably impaired."[144] The power of the moral example is diminished if the moral perfection of the Exemplar is guaranteed by his divinity, and the corollary of an exemplarist theory of the Atonement is a purely human life of Christ, for "clearly the more closely that life conforms to the ordinary human conditions the greater will be its hold upon mankind".[145] The drift, then, of the Broad Church scheme was towards a Unitarian view of Christ, and in the nineteenth century the abandonment of the substitutionary view of the Atonement, as of the doctrine of everlasting punishment, was frequently the precursor of the adoption of Unitarianism. It is not suggested that all Broad Churchmen were weak on the divinity of Christ. But the divinity of a Christ whose miracles are accounted for largely in naturalistic terms[146] and whose atoning work consists chiefly in the power of his moral example is in jeopardy; and there is some evidence of a certain loosening of the hold of Broad Churchmen on the divinity of Christ. Not that this was entirely the consequence of the adoption of the foregoing views—rather both it and they were the result of a rationalistic yet sensitive approach to religious problems.

It remains to give some examples of the tendency among certain Broad Churchmen towards a more Unitarian view of Christ. That there was such a tendency may be seen from the frank admission of F. W. Robertson that "unquestionably, the belief in the Divinity of Christ is waning among us".[147] "They who hold it," he said, "have petrified it into a theological dogma without life or warmth, and thoughtful men are more and more beginning to put it aside."[148] Robertson's own solution to the problem was to try to "lay the foundations of a higher faith deeply in a belief of His Humanity"[149]—which can hardly have been very reassuring to more orthodox Churchmen, particularly when he cited Dr. Channing, the Unitarian, as possessing the requisite "personal love and adoration of Christ" in which "the Christian religion consists".[150]

The opponents of the Broad Churchmen were often, in fact, far more percipient of the drift of the latter's teaching than were the Broad Churchmen themselves. Thus E. B. Pusey wrote in reply to an appeal to the "common Christianity" between himself and Benjamin Jowett: "Alas I do not know what single truth we hold in common, except that somehow Jesus came from God, which the Mohammedans believe too. I do not think that Professor Jowett believes our Lord to have been Very God, or God the Holy Ghost to be a Personal Being."[151] And that Pusey's fears for Jowett's orthodoxy were not groundless may be seen, for example, from Jowett's statement that "definite statements respecting the relation of Christ either to God or man are only figures of speech",[152] or from the following extract from a sermon on Christ's unity with the Father. "The creed tells us", says Jowett, "that He was 'equal to the Father as touching His Godhead, inferior to the Father as touching His manhood'. But is it not more intelligible to us, and more instructive, to think of Him as one with God, because Christ and God are one with righteousness and truth? Christ does not so much assume to be God as he naturally loses Himself in God. . . . The confidence of Christ is . . . not confidence in self, but absolute dependence on the will of God. He has no fear, except one and for a moment, lest He should be forsaken by God."[153] Similar doubts might have been entertained regarding H. R. Haweis, when he wrote: "We cannot say of Christ that He exhausted in His person the possibilities of God; but we can say

76

that He was true God in the same way that a drop of sea water is true ocean, although the ocean hath within it possibilities and functions beyond the drop of sea water."[154] And fears regarding Colenso's orthodoxy were hardly likely to be allayed when, in the course of a sermon on the Lord's Prayer, he made the same point as Dr. Samuel Clarke and the Unitarian Theophilus Lindsey had, in the eighteenth century, made before him, viz., that worship and prayer should be addressed, not to Christ, but to the Father alone. Current devotional practice was erroneous in offering direct worship to Christ, and *Hymns Ancient and Modern* contained, Colenso urged, "Many expressions which would have been utterly condemned by our Lord and His apostles, expressions in which not only is adoration paid to Jesus instead of to 'our Father and His Father', to 'our God and His God', but the very thorns and cross and nails . . . are called upon to satisfy our spirits, to fill us with love, to plant in our souls the root of virtue, and mature its glorious fruit. But, indeed, the whole book overflows with words of prayer and praise, directly addressed to Jesus, such as find no example or warrant in the lessons of our Lord Himself, nor in the language of His apostles."[155] This, it may be urged, was merely a return to Scriptural usage, but it was on the basis of a similar return to Scriptural usage that the Arianism of the eighteenth century was produced; and it is difficult not to feel that, reflected in Colenso's words, in spite of his protestations of orthodoxy, there is at least an incipient Arianism.

It was, in fact, on the basis of a similar return to Scriptural authority that Liddon's Bampton Lectures on *The Divinity of Christ* were attacked in 1871 by an anonymous "clergyman of the Church of England"[156] who found himself "unable to escape the conclusion, that the dogma Mr. Liddon advocates is false".[157] The dogma might be maintained on the basis of ecclesiastical authority, he thought, but "in enforced association with Protestantism, it is totally out of place; and whatever advantages may attend it elsewhere, its imposition as an Article of Faith within the Churches of the Reformation, is unwarranted and demoralizing".[158]

Charles Voysey declared in *The Sling and the Stone* that "the Lord Jesus Christ is no more very God of very God than we men are; that the worship of Christ is idolatry and inconsistent with the worship of the true God".[159] The expression of these views, particularly in so extreme a form, naturally cost Voysey ejection from the Church of England, but he claimed to be saying only what other Broad Churchmen were saying in more general terms.[160]

Stopford Brooke also left the Church of England, though voluntarily, for disbelief in, besides other doctrines, the orthodox doctrine of the divinity of Christ. And signs of the weakening of its hold upon him were not lacking long before the final break came. Thus, eight years before his secession, Brooke wrote in 1872 of his sermons of the previous year: "It strikes me, almost painfully, that my sermons have been far more Theistic than Christian, and that Christ has nearly altogether disappeared from them."[161]

In view of the foregoing, and the Unitarian acknowledgement of Jesus as their spiritual leader,[162] it is perhaps not surprising that when discussing in 1886 the possibility of closing the gap between Unitarianism and his own church Canon W. H. Fremantle should say: "Nor as to the position assigned to our Lord, is it clear that the fundamental difference which is usually assumed exists. For what is the practical meaning of the divinity of Christ? It is this, that we accept him as morally supreme, that our consciences acknowledge the absolute dominion of his nature and spirit."[163] And regarding this confession of moral supremacy he added: "We shall find none who make this confession more heartily than do many of the Unitarians, and none who translate this confession into practice more sincerely."[164]

The Affinity shown in the Use of Traditional Language, in Liturgical Practice, and in Architectural Style

In spite of the liberal character of much of their thinking neither the Unitarians nor the Broad Churchmen were entirely radical. Both exhibited conservative tendencies, which, particularly on the Unitarian side, had the effect of increasing the similarity between them.

The conservatism of the Broad Churchmen expressed itself in their employment of the traditional forms of worship, as prescribed in the *Book of Common Prayer*. This, of course, along with the use of traditional Church buildings, as opposed to buildings of the "meeting-house" or "chapel" style, was the inevitable result of the fact that the Broad Churchmen were Anglicans and as such committed to the use of these patterns and components of worship. But it must not be assumed from this that the Broad Churchmen were reluctant Anglicans; and there is no evidence of any desire on their part to change the essential style or framework of their worship: even Charles Voysey, who when forced to leave the Anglican fold, retained, after his founding of the "Theistic Church",[1] the clerical garb of an Anglican Clergyman,[2] and based his own liturgy on the *Book of Common Prayer*.[3] The Broad Churchmen were uneasy, however, about the Athanasian Creed;[4] and the Apostles' and Nicene Creeds and the Thirty-Nine Articles were often understood in a sophisticated sense, which to many Unitarians seemed not entirely ingenuous. To the latter, in fact, this public profession of the ancient formularies by men of known theological radicalism was something of a scandal. And though the Unitarians could not but admire the liberalizing tendency of the presence of such men as Jowett and Stanley in the Anglican church they were yet worried about their moral position. Thus *The Inquirer*, in reference to certain conclusions of Jowett and other Broad Churchmen found it "difficult to reconcile these conclusions with the ecclesiastical position of the Broad Church theologians and their retention of emoluments held on the condition of assenting to formularies which it is the whole tendency of their writings to disprove";[5] and James Martineau "thought that men like Dean Stanley ought to have seceded from the Established Church".[6] This, moreover, was not inconsistent with Martineau's desire to broaden the church, for while "he considered it eminently desirable to alter the formularies, so as to admit many who are now excluded . . . until they have been altered, he reckoned it wrong and almost dishonest for those to remain in the church who question many of the doctrines expressed in its rather narrow and rigid creeds and other documents".[7]

The practice of the Broad Churchmen, then, involved the use of terminology which had to be understood in a refined and somewhat unnatural sense, and to the Unitarian conscience this seemed insincere. But an examination of Unitarian writings shows that Unitarians also were not guiltless in this respect. Thus, for example, James Martineau, during the course of some correspondence with Dr. Sadler regarding the *Common Prayer for Christian Worship*,[8] in the production of which he took part, wrote in 1861: "My scruple about the terms 'Mediator', 'Redeemer', and 'Saviour' applied to Christ, has always lingered and hung about my mind from boyhood, though I am ashamed to say I have never till now had the courage and simplicity to look it fairly in the face. And now that I do so, and try the hearts of others on the matter, I find that they too suffer from the same feeling of misleading profession and infirm sincerity in the use of these words which has secretly troubled me all my life";[9] and regarding such interpretations to which he and other Unitarians subjected the above-mentioned terms, he admitted that while they "provide an intelligible meaning" for them "it is . . . indubitably an *invented* meaning, devised in order to save the phrases,—and *not* by any means the sense they bear either in scripture whence they come, or in the Church which has fixed their permanent significance".[10] Yet only about twenty years before this he had included in his *Hymns for the Christian Church and Home* (1840), in the section allotted to "Christ and Christianity", which comprised seventy-three hymns, no less than eighteen hymns employing the terms "Saviour" or "Redeemer" in respect of Jesus—about 25 per cent of the whole.[11] Nor did the term "Saviour", with the same reference, disappear from his *Hymns of Praise and Prayer* published in 1874.[12] Indeed, in spite of Martineau's protestation that for this soteriological language with its implicit idea of "a transference from a prior lost or enslaved to a subsequent rescued condition"[13] he could "see nothing for it but rejection",[14] he included in his contribution to *Common Prayer for Christian Worship* —about which the previously mentioned correspondence took place—the following passage, which clearly expresses the very concept he rejected:

"The Son of God hath dwelt among us: full of grace and truth;
The Son of Man hath gone up on high: made perfect through
    suffering for the holy of holies.
He is our peace: giving us access by one spirit to the Father
No more strangers and exiles: but fellow-citizens with the saints,
    and of the household of God".[15]

However Martineau might interpret this passage he was certainly laying himself open to the charge of making a "misleading profession".

There are, in fact, some[16] who see in the troubled face of Martineau's later years[17] a reflection of the conflict in the mind of a man whose devotional expression was not entirely in harmony with his rationalistic theology—a man who, in spite of his Broad Church theological sympathy, could yet confess in respect of his capacity as an editor of a hymn book "offered to a Nonconformist Broad Church" that his "prevailing feeling carries him less to Broad Church sources than to other springs,— Catholic, Mystical, semi-Puritan, Lutheran, Wesleyan,—and gives him therefore what he most loves, and what speaks most truly for him, mingled with much that neither he nor his readers can believe".[18]

More significant, however, from the specifically Anglican aspect of the Unitarian and Broad Church affinity than this attempt to re-interpret traditional phraseology was the not unrelated fact that to quite a remarkable extent Unitarian liturgies were based upon the *Book of Common Prayer*.

The use of a liturgy at all was something of a novelty, for the Nonconformist churches in England have never been particularly attracted to set prayers,[19] and perhaps naturally so as it was largely through refusal to accept the Prayer Book of 1662, with the resultant Toleration Act of 1689,[20] that Nonconformity came to be established in this country. No English Nonconformist liturgy can be traced before 1753,[21] and from then on, till the end of the eighteenth century, all the liturgies that can be found were either Arian or Unitarian in their theology.[22] The influence of Dr. Samuel Clarke's revision of the *Book of Common Prayer* in this connection has already been noted in the first chapter.

In the nineteenth century this general pattern continued. Unitarians were almost the only English Nonconformists to use liturgies as a normal pattern of worship,[23] which in itself is indicative of "a very real yearning for a degree of order and ritual more usually associated with the Church of England".[24] But what is more important is the fact that the majority of the liturgies employed were modelled on the *Book of Common Prayer*.

Between 1801 and 1900 Unitarians in England produced about fifty-six liturgies,[25] of which only six were not based on the *Book of Common Prayer*.[26] None of the latter, moreover, went into a second edition, whereas more than a quarter of those based on the *Book of Common Prayer* went into second, and some into many, editions.[27] Three nineteenth-century editions of eighteenth-century liturgies, all based, or containing services based, on the *Book of Common Prayer* were also produced.[28] Thus the *Book of Common Prayer* affected roughly 90 per cent of the liturgies in use by Unitarians in the nineteenth century.

A detailed examination is not called for, but it will be of

interest to make a brief analysis of the contents of the first service in *Common Prayer for Christian Worship*, which latter was probably the most influential and widely used Unitarian prayer book of the nineteenth century.[29] The service begins with Sentences, only one of which is not in the *Book of Common Prayer*. These are followed by the Exhortation and General Confession—the latter slightly modified by the omission of the phrases "and there is no health in us" and "miserable offenders". There being no Absolution, the Lord's Prayer comes next, along with an attenuated form of the Versicles and Responses. The *Gloria Patri* is omitted *passim*. Then follow a shortened form of the *Venite*, the First Lesson, and an abbreviated version of the *Te Deum* from which a number of orthodox phrases have been cut, though there are references to the Son and the Holy Spirit. As in the *Book of Common Prayer*, the *Benedicite* is given as an alternative, but is here shortened. Then follows the Second Lesson, along with the *Benedictus*, and the *Jubilate Deo* as an alternative. Both are abbreviated. The Apostles' Creed, which appears at this point in the Anglican Service, is omitted, along with the Suffrages, the Lord's Prayer, and Versicles. Then follow the Collect for the Day, an abridged form of the Collect for Peace, and the Collect for Grace. The Prayer for the King's Majesty follows, minus the reference to the vanquishing of enemies, along with the Prayer for the Royal Family and the Prayer for Clergy and people, both of the latter being also slightly amended. Then follow the Prayer for the High Court of Parliament, the Prayer for all Conditions of men, and the General Thanksgiving—all of which are subjected to only a minimum of alteration. Then follows a prayer in commemoration of the faithful departed, which is not found in the *Book of Common Prayer*. The service ends with a revised form of the Prayer of St. Chrysostom, and the Benediction from 2 Corinthians 13, with that in Philippians 4 as an alternative.

As may be seen from the foregoing, the service is but a revised form of the order for Morning Prayer in the Anglican Prayer Book. The second service stands in a similar relationship to the Anglican order for Evening Prayer, and though the subsequent services are not so closely based on the *Book of Common Prayer*, the influence of the latter is clearly discernible, as also in the fact that the book contains such features as services for the Baptism of Infants, the Baptism of those of Riper Years, Confirmation, and Prayers to be used at Sea. Quite clearly many Unitarians could say, as stated in the preface of one of their liturgies, that they took "a sincere pleasure in adopting a mode of worship" which lessened "the distance between them and their brethren of the 'establishment' ".[30]

But an Anglican style of worship needs an Anglican type of setting for worship, and this leads naturally to a consideration of another, though rather less important, point of similarity between Unitarianism and the Anglican Broad Church, viz., the ready manner in which Unitarians adopted Gothic architecture as the appropriate style for their church buildings.

Considering the fact of their Puritan heritage of box-like chapels, on the one hand, and the radical nature of their theological thinking on the other it is surprising that the Unitarians adopted such a traditional style. But it was the Anglican style, and it suited their Anglican mode of worship.

The revival of Gothic architecture in the nineteenth century for church buildings in England was, of course, part of a much wider movement, the discussion of which falls outside the scope of this book,[31] but its popularity owed something not only to its economic[32] advantages, but also to its romantic, theological, and "ecclesiological"[33] associations and significance. But whatever its associations on the Continent, or in books on ecclesiology, for most people in England in the nineteenth century, as probably even for most people today, the Gothic style of architecture was, and is, particularly "Anglican". It is the style in which so many of the older Anglican churches are built, and just as the box-like structures of a Nonconformist chapel signifies "Congregationalist", "Baptist", etc., so, for most people, the Gothic style signifies "Anglican", and it comes as something of a surprise to find that a church constructed in such a style is not Anglican.

When Gothic revival in church building began about 1818

it was naturally the Anglicans who were the first to take it up;[34] and a third of a century was to pass before Nonconformity in general came to adopt it, and this is not surprising as it did not suit their non-liturgical form of service. But for Unitarians this was not the case, and thus they came to build churches in the Gothic style rather earlier than most Nonconformists.[35] As early as 1839 a church designed by Sir Charles Barry, the architect of the Houses of Parliament, was built for the congregation of J. J. Tayler at Upper Brook Street, Manchester; and it was fully Gothic, except for the fact that, in accordance with the Nonconformist emphasis on preaching, the pulpit stood in the middle of the end wall, instead of an altar. Others quickly followed, such as Dukinfield (1840) and St. Petersgate, Stockport (1842). But the first Nonconformist church known to have an altar in the chancel, so emphasizing the devotional aspect of worship, and a closer association with Anglicanism, was at Gee Cross, Hyde (1848),[36] followed by Mill Hill, Leeds, in the same year, Hope Street Church, Liverpool (1849), Christ Church, Banbury (1850) and Bank Street, Bury (1852),— in all of which cases the influence of the finally more dominant wing of Unitarianism, which emphasized its breadth, and its affinity with the National Church, is to be seen. Thereafter a flood of Unitarian Gothic followed, and it is not for nothing that in A. L. Drummond's *The Church Architecture of Protestantism* it is a Unitarian church, viz., the Old Meeting, Birmingham (1885), that is described as "a landmark in Nonconformist Church Architecture".[37] Some idea of the Unitarian predilection for this style may be gathered from the fact that in the Unitarian booklet, *The Churches and Chapels of the East Cheshire Christian Union*,[38] of the thirteen churches listed as having been built between 1840 and 1879, only three, and one of these a Sunday school and mission, do not show the influence of Gothic, and some, as, for example, Gee Cross, and Flowery Field, Hyde, can only be described as fully Gothic;[39] and around the middle of the century, in a number of places, as, for example, Kingswood, Leicester, and Warwick, even ancient meeting houses were altered, by the provision of a chancel and altar, in accordance with the move towards Gothic, and more Anglican ways of worship.

For some High Church Anglicans, with their interest in ecclesiology, the use of such symbolic architecture by any "congregation of Socinians" involved the prostitution of "the speaking architecture of the Church" in "the service of her bitterest enemies".[40] But it must not be thought from this that the High Churchmen were the only Anglicans who were interested in Gothic. That interest, though not in the narrow ecclesiological sense, belonged to the Anglican Church as a whole, and not least to the Broad Churchmen, whose great spokesman, Dean Stanley, saw in "the recovery, the second birth, of Gothic architecture" a striking proof that "the human mind is not dead, nor the power of our Maker slackened".[41] For him, as for the Unitarians, Gothic made its religious appeal because of "its sobriety, its grandeur, its breadth, its sublimity";[42] and for them, as for Dr. Arnold, there was a persistent hope that the influence of Anglican ideals would rescue their church buildings from the "utter coarseness and deformity"[43] that the great Broad Churchman saw in the church architecture of Nonconformity.

CHAPTER 5

The Affinity shown in Mutual Interaction

It has now been seen that there was a considerable similarity both of approach and of general character between Unitarianism and the Anglican Broad Church; and it remains to consider what evidence there is of mutual interaction. Mutual influence is, of course, not an easy matter to trace since some of the most potent influences in life frequently work unconsciously; and, further, it may reasonably be assumed that for sheer reasons of diplomacy[1] reticence rather than open acknowledgement would be the characteristic attitude of Broad Churchmen regarding any influence coming from Unitarian sources.[2] Moreover, it must surely be conceded as not unlikely that the orthodox historians, on whom to a very large extent research is dependent in this matter, would, in view of the generally hostile attitude towards Unitarianism, tend to minimize or cover any such influence.[3]

That there was some cross influence is suggested not only by the similarities already observed, but also because some of the protagonists of the Broad Church had either a Unitarian background, or were the sort of persons to whom both Unitarianism and the Broad Church could appeal, or again because they actually became Unitarians. In the first category F. D. Maurice should be placed, in the second Samuel Taylor Coleridge, and in the third Stopford Brooke. Examination of these and other facts clearly demonstrate, though in varying degree, a noteworthy measure of cross influence, particularly from the Unitarian side. It will be convenient to begin with a consideration of the three personalities already mentioned, and to take them in chronological order.

87

S. T. Coleridge became a Unitarian while an undergraduate at Cambridge in 1793 under the influence of his tutor, W. Frend,[4] who belonged to the company of ex-Anglican Latitudinarians with whom the name of Theophilus Lindsey and the Feathers Tavern Petition are associated.

The Unitarian phase of Coleridge's religious life lasted not much more than a decade,[5] but within that period he was—to use his own description of himself—"a zealous Unitarian in religion".[6] For Joseph Priestley he shared with Charles Lamb an almost idolatrous admiration,[7] and referred to him in his *Religious Musings* as "patriot, saint, and sage";[8] and he formed an especial friendship with John Estlin, the minister of the Unitarian congregation at Lewin's Mead, Bristol, who "during the early part of Coleridge's career . . . exercised a remarkable influence over him".[9] He preached at a number of Unitarian churches in various parts of the country, including such important churches as New Meeting, Birmingham, of which Priestley had previously been minister, and the High Pavement Chapel, Nottingham;[10] and Cottle refers to Coleridge's being "strongly recommended"[11] to offer himself as a minister.

In 1798 he preached at Shrewsbury with a view to becoming Unitarian minister there, and though as a result of an annuity being settled upon him by Thomas and Josiah Wedgwood—both Unitarians—he decided against the acceptance of a regular pulpit, he continued to preach elsewhere, and in a letter declared: "I have a humble trust, that many years will not pass over my head before I shall have given proof in some way or other that active zeal for Unitarian Christianity, not indolence or indifference, has been the motive of my declining a local and stated settlement as preacher of it."[12] In 1802 he wrote to Estlin: "If there be any meaning in words, it appears to me that the Quakers and Unitarians are the only Christians," though he added that "some of the Unitarians make too much an *Idol* of their *one* God".[13]

Coleridge soon found, however,—as did James Martineau later—that the materialistic philosophy of Hartley, which "as interpreted by Priestley had practically entire command of the

Unitarian field"[14] at that time, was profoundly unsatisfying; and after a period of study in Germany developed the philosophy which led to his recovery of Trinitarian belief which came in 1807. Even so, however, Coleridge could still say in a letter to Estlin at the close of 1808, "I believe the Father of all to be the only Object of Adoration or Prayer", and describe the difference between himself and the Unitarian minister as "rather philosophical than theological".[15] Thus, as John Hunt declared, "The defection of Coleridge from the Unitarians was more a rebellion against Unitarian philosophy than against Unitarian theology."[16]

Coleridge went on to have a profound religious influence, particularly in the Anglican Broad Church,[17] where his views on the inspiration of the Bible, the nature of the Church, his attitude to science, and his stand for freedom of thought in religion[18] as opposed to a too-ready acceptance of authority were especially pervasive. The rationalistic streak in him which attracted him to Unitarianism, and which was doubtless stimulated in him during his Unitarian period, still continued to manifest itself, and though he formally accepted orthodox doctrines, he frequently gave them a rationalistic interpretation—such as became characteristic of Broad Church writers—which minimized their difficulties, while preserving as far as possible their moral and religious truth.[19] Thus, for example, he treated the epithet "original" involved in the doctrine of Original Sin as a pleonasm, and contended that sin as a spiritual evil was not inherited from without, but was an act of the will itself.[20] How far such an interpretation was the result of Unitarian influence —Unitarians had long been opposed to the doctrine of Original Sin—it is impossible to determine, but it is certain that no Unitarian would have wished to deny the truth that Coleridge therein wished to convey. Nor could Coleridge have been truer to his Unitarian past when he wrote: "If Reason justly contradicts an article, it is not of the household of Faith";[21] or when he frequently observed: "I do not so much care for men's religious opinions—they vary, and are dependant (sic) on that which usually surrounds them—but I regard with more attention what men are."[22] For such were characteristic Unitarian positions. The same may also be said of Coleridge's concern for liberty, and of his view that "the mistakes of scientific men have never injured Christianity, while every new truth discovered by them has either added to its evidence or prepared the mind for its reception".[23] Unitarians were particularly ready to welcome the results of science, and there can be little doubt that part of the attraction which Joseph Priestley had for the youthful Coleridge consisted in his great ability as a scientist.[24] Between Coleridge the Unitarian and Coleridge the Trinitarian there may be seen much similarity and continuing influence, and it is certainly not without significance with regard to that influence that he who was hailed by the Unitarians as "the rising star of their society"[25] earned for himself the title of "Father of the Broad Church Movement".[26]

F. D. Maurice was the son of a Unitarian minister, and thus, though the members of the household in which his formative years were spent were not united in their views on religion— the mother and three sisters seceded from the father's faith, though not to become members of the same church—the predominant influence during Maurice's early years was Unitarian; and, indeed, at the close of his Cambridge career he refused to take his degree rather than declare himself a member of the Church of England. Only a few years were to elapse, however, before he became a member of the Established Church, in which he became so distinguished a figure. But no man can entirely escape the influence of his early environment, and there are features in the teaching of Maurice on which a knowledge of his Unitarian past can throw an interesting light.

While it cannot be proved that Maurice's opposition to the doctrine of eternal punishment in its normally accepted sense was entirely the result of his Unitarian upbringing, the influence of that background must surely have done something more than merely have facilitated the development of such a repudiation. For whereas the rejection of the doctrine of eternal punishment was characteristic of Unitarianism, it was something of a heresy in the Church of England in the time of Maurice, and the fact that he had been a Unitarian strongly suggests that his views on the subject are ultimately traceable to his Unitarian past. "I was brought up in the belief of universal restitution", wrote Maurice in a letter to F. J. A. Hort, "I was taught that the idea of eternal punishment could not consist with the goodness and mercy of God"; and he went on to add, "I despised the Universalist and Unitarian as weak; I do not know that I found anything at all better."[27]

Another interesting matter consists in Maurice's attraction for the concept of the Fatherhood of God. Mrs. George Boole, who had a fairly intimate acquaintance with Maurice, declared that for Maurice "the word *Father* itself certainly had . . . some meaning and associations which it might not have for others", and that in spiritual matters the Fatherhood of God was a supreme concept for Maurice, for he gave indications that "he had nothing to tell anybody which that word (Father) did not convey".[28] While it may be that the great importance of the concept for Maurice was in some measure due to the influence of his own father, as Mrs. Boole suggests when she asks "What *can* there have been in the elder Maurice to make the word *Father* mean so much to his son that all other words have lost their meaning?",[29] yet the more likely source of this attachment is surely the Unitarianism in which he was brought up, and which concentrated worship upon the Father rather than upon the Son. For, even though, as H. G. Wood says, Maurice's reaction to the belief in the Fatherhood of God as he had learned it in Unitarianism was that he found "the doctrine as presented to him, too shallow",[30] the fact remains that this was the earliest—and therefore it is to be concluded, no doubt, the most influential—way in which Maurice had been led to think about God, and constituted the focus of his youthful religious devotion.

It is, furthermore, surely not illegitimate to see in Maurice's opposition to the substitutionary view of the Atonement an evidence of the continuing influence of his Unitarian past, which had a long history of opposition to the traditional understanding of the doctrine. Again, in the decidedly liberal attitude towards non-Christian religions which Maurice adopted in his Boyle Lecture, *The Religions of the World,*[31] which lecture Powicke writing in 1930 considered probably "did more than anything else to inspire the new attitude towards the non-Christian world"[32] there may be seen something of the more liberal attitude of Unitarians towards non-Christian religions, as exemplified in their attitude towards Rammohun Roy, "the morning star of Hindoo reformation",[33] for example, and also of the universalism in which Maurice had been brought up. Moreover, though it was from Thomas Erskine,[34] and not, of course, from Unitarianism, that Maurice derived his doctrine that Christ is the head of the whole human race, and that all are in some sense members of the Church,[35] whether or not they recognize themselves to be such, it would be strange if the latter doctrine, viz., universalism, did not facilitate the acceptance of such a conception. It is interesting, furthermore, that Maurice's concept of man as being "in Christ" instead of being—as he was so commonly regarded in orthodox eyes—"in Adam",[36] unless regenerate, brought him into closer line with Unitarian thought, which rejected the idea of original sin. Again in his opposition to theological system-making[37] it is perhaps not too much to see something of the influence of his father who was "not a hard dogmatic Unitarian" and who in the matter of his use of the Trinitarian baptismal formula "was not concerned to harmonise his practice with the divinity he had learnt at Hoxton".[38]

While on the subject of Maurice, it is interesting, furthermore, to note that some of Maurice's contemporaries were sensitive to a Unitarian tendency in him. Thus Liddon writing in a letter to Dean Stanley, in which he declined an invitation to preach at Westminster Abbey because Maurice had also been similarly invited, declared of Maurice: "That he is so good a man I rejoice to believe with all my heart. It is an earnest of his return to the Church. That so good a man should be mistaken is a very perplexing mystery of the moral world. . . . But *mere* moral goodness is not a sufficient basis for engaging in a public profession to teach people a common faith. You must draw the line somewhere; and the question is one of degree. No one doubts Channing's goodness. Yet Channing taught Socinianism in terms."[39] Evidently, for Liddon, Maurice might in some measure be compared with Channing; and only a little more than a year beforehand Liddon had been partly instrumental in preventing the ordination of Walter Pater, whose "perusal of the works of Maurice . . . gradually led him to become a doubter".[40] Edward White, another of Maurice's contemporaries, held a similar view of the effect of Maurice's works, and F. J. Powicke records that he was "very emphatic, not to say truculent in his assertion of his belief that its chief effect was to produce Unitarians".[41] "It is never to be forgotten", wrote White, "that Maurice's doctrine was a growth out of Unitarianism (congenital), and was a movement towards orthodoxy —a sort of half-way house towards orthodoxy—specially helpful to a Unitarian on his travels towards the Heavenly Jerusalem. It has preserved many from Unitarianism, I doubt not. There is, however, a double use for a road—towards the Heavenly Jerusalem and away from it, and my point is, that while many have travelled . . . along this road upwards, there are others who—starting from orthodoxy (or Evangelicalism) have gone in the other direction, and descended through Mauriceanism into Unitarianism of a rather virulent description—all the worse for their previous history."[42]

But perhaps the best testimony to the Unitarian influence at work in Maurice is to be found in his own words regarding his Unitarian upbringing. "I now deliberately regard it", he said, in a letter written in 1866, "as one of the great mercies of my life that I had this birth and the education which belonged to it. . . . My ends have been shaped for me, rough hew them how I would, and shape has been given to them by my father's function and this name 'Unitarian' more than by any other influences, though I have been exposed to many of the most different kind which have strangely affected and may appear to some to have entirely disturbed that primary one."[43] Though he found it necessary to abandon his original faith he could still say, "I have found in many of the Unitarian body whom I have known and do know, Divine Graces which I have not found in myself . . . ,"[44] which was a bold declaration to make when discussing the Athanasian Creed in 1862, as also to add that "the Unitarian may be much nearer the Kingdom of Heaven than we are. He may in very deed less divide the substance, less confound the persons, than we do".[45]

Stopford Brooke was a prominent Broad Church author and preacher. His *Life and Letters of the Late Frederick W. Robertson*, published in 1865, "was recognised as a work of exceptional power, and of great importance as a broad church document",[46] and as a preacher in London he drew large congregations. In 1867 he became chaplain-in-ordinary to Queen Victoria, who was a patron of the Broad Church.[47]

Though it was not until 1880 that he finally broke with the Church of England, Brooke was early the subject of Unitarian influence. Originally he had been an Evangelical, and though the causes of his movement from the Evangelical position to that of the Broad Church were several, among them must be placed the writings of R. W. Emerson, the Unitarian, whose *Essays* he read and discussed night after night while at college.[48] He was familiar also at this stage with Emerson's *Address to the Senior Class in Divinity College*,[49] wherein Emerson asserts that one of the chief defects of historical Christianity is that "It has dwelt, it dwells, with noxious exaggeration about the *person* of Jesus", and goes on to declare regarding Jesus that "The manner in which his name is surrounded with expressions, which were once sallies of admiration and love, but are now petrified into official titles, kills all generous sympathy and liking. All who hear me feel that the language that describes Christ to Europe and America, is not the style of friendship and enthusiasm to a good and noble heart, but is appropriated and formal,—paints a demi-god as the Orientals or the Greeks would describe Osiris or Apollo".[50] When L. P. Jacks, Brooke's biographer, in summarizing Brooke's Christological position as expressed in the first volume of his published sermons (1869), declares that "The outstanding feature is an intense human love for Christ as a personality—as a man. . . . Every form of thought which by exalting his divinity places a gulf between

Christ and Man is immediately swept away or dissolved into some other form in which the original features of the dogma are completely lost"[51] something of the effect of his early reading may, surely, be seen. In a sermon preached in 1871 Brooke declared: "I have a great affection and respect for the genius of Emerson. Few men have such a kindly power, few suggest so much. He *does* disturb the mind to healthy questioning, and open to it new paths."[52]

Martineau, however, seems to have been the main Unitarian influence upon Brooke. Thus extracts from Brooke's diary, quoted by his biographer, indicate that as early as 1857, when he was twenty-five, Brooke was reading Martineau,[53] and not long afterwards he was saying to his friends that "a man might learn something from Martineau".[54] His diary for 1859 reveals that he is still studying the same writer, and he advises a friend to read him, and "see if a Unitarian cannot teach and comfort somewhat".[55] Nor was this teaching lost on Brooke. In 1861 Martineau wrote: "The Incarnation is true not of Christ exclusively, but of Man universally and God everlastingly,"[56] and in 1867 Brooke declared: "The whole of humanity is penetrated by the Divine. This is the foundation stone of the Gospel of Christ . . . and we call it the Incarnation."[57]

How important, in fact, Martineau was in Brooke's thinking may be judged from the question he asked Dean Stanley when discussing the envisaged broadening of the Church of England, viz., "Will it broaden sufficiently to admit James Martineau being made Archbishop of Canterbury?", and his avowal of his intention to leave the Church when he received the reply: "Not in our time."[58]

Brooke subsequently became—to use his own phrase in description of himself—"a leading Unitarian",[59] but his secession from the Church of England in 1880 involved no radical change in his teaching, and he continued to preach in the same proprietary chapel and to much the same congregation as he had in his later Broad Church days. But the change brought one most significant addition to his congregation—the aged James Martineau,[60] who was to continue as a member until Brooke's own retirement, and of whom in a Memorial Address in 1900 Brooke declared: "Even the Church of England, with its cry 'Can any good thing come out of the Unitarian Village', has been goaded into dim confessions of his use. On the whole, I have no doubt that the battle is practically won against the forces of godless science and godless ethics, and that Martineau has been the best builder, among many others, of a religion bound up with Jesus Christ, rooted in the confession of the Fatherhood of God, which is agreeable to reason, and in full accordance with the ethical progress of man in history."[61]

Among the influences upon Stopford Brooke must be reckoned the distinguished Anglican Broad Church preacher, F. W. Robertson,[62] who again, interestingly enough was the subject of Unitarian influence, and also, like Brooke, was helped in his passage from an Evangelical to a Broad Church position by a study of Unitarian writings.

One of the most important influences upon Robertson was James Martineau, and in particular his *Endeavours after the Christian Life*.[63] J. Hoatson, after a careful study of Robertson's sermons, declared that "examination reveals traces of the influence of 37 out of the 43 sermons in the *Endeavours* upon at least 62 of the 125 published sermons of Robertson".[64] These sixty-two Hoatson analyses as follows: "(1) Seven, which could not have been what they are had the *Endeavours* not been written. (2) Twenty-five, in which there is either strong general resemblances, or debt incurred either in one long or several shorter passages. (3) Thirty, where the resemblance, though slight, is distinct, or where there is at least one short passage, the inspiration of which is undoubted."[65] Much of this extraordinary influence may be attributed to the indirect effect of the thoroughness of Robertson's reading—"I will answer for it", he said, "that there are few girls of eighteen who have not read more books than I have; and as to religious books, I could count upon my fingers in two minutes all I ever read—but they are mine"[66]—but that there was much conscious borrowing may be seen from extracts quoted in the notes[67]—a fact which is emphasized by his complaint that "the perpetual treadmill necessity of being for ever ready twice a week with earnest thoughts on solemn subjects is a task which is quite enough to break down all originality, and convert a racehorse into a dray".[68] This must not be taken to mean, however, that Martineau's influence was discontinuous and based on mere expediency. Robertson was a noble soul, and his use of Martineau until the last year of his life in 1853 was based upon a spiritual affinity with him. "It was in the great crises of his life and ministry, when his nature was most deeply stirred and the heaviest demands were made upon it, when especially he required the consolation, the uplift, the inspirations of the divinest thought, that he turned to the teacher who, next to the great Master Himself, most fully satisfied the cravings of his soul."[69]

Just when the Unitarian influence upon Robertson began it is impossible to determine precisely, but it is not unlikely that Robertson's initial interest in Unitarianism was aroused, when he became curate to Archibald Boyd, the Evangelical rector at Cheltenham in the summer of 1842. The tiny Unitarian cause which had begun in Cheltenham in a layman's "parlour" only a decade before[70] was growing in strength and beginning to attract hostile notice. Frances Power Cobbe, who later became a Unitarian, referring to this time declared: "I can remember Mr. Boyd about this period preaching at Cheltenham, and denouncing the Unitarians with such singular vehemence, that it induced me to institute careful enquiries concerning a body of whose tenets at that time I was in total ignorance";[71] and, though Frances Cobbe notes that "Robertson was at first in full harmony with Mr. Boyd's opinions",[72] it would not be surprising if this vigorous attack on Unitarianism did not produce in Robertson a reaction similar to that in Frances Cobbe.

The first clear evidence of Robertson's contact with Unitarianism after this, however, belongs to the year 1846 during his brief residence at Heidelberg, when, as Robertson's biographer states, "his six weeks' stay in this place led to a large correspondence afterwards; especially on the part of some Unitarians, who, struck by his tolerance . . . wished to hear more from him on the subject of their controversy".[73]

D   97

During 1843 and the following years, however, Robertson's biographer records that "doubts and questionings began to stir in his mind" under the influence of "his reading and his intercourse with men",[74] so that he was no longer an Evangelical; and, observing the fact that Martineau's *Endeavours* was published in the summer of 1843, Hoatson makes the suggestion that the latter may well have been included in the "reading" which helped to produce the change[75]—a suggestion which has still greater cogency in the light of the events of 1842 and 1846. Thus Boyd's anti-Unitarian preaching, or the situation which caused Boyd to preach in this way, would arouse Robertson's interest in Unitarianism and so predispose him to read the distinguished Unitarian's sermons when they were published some months later, and which reading would help to account for the "tolerance" and "atoning influence"[76] which Robertson exhibited during his contacts with the Unitarians at Heidelberg in 1846.

However that may be, the first trace of Martineau's influence in Robertson's sermons occurs in June and July of 1847, in two discourses entitled respectively "The Christian's Hope and Destiny Hereafter" and "The Kingdom of Heaven", both of which reveal indebtedness to Martineau's two sermons entitled "The Kingdom of God within us";[77] and it is not unlikely that the cause of this is to be found in the Heidelberg episode of the previous autumn, when—a fact which his biographer does not mention—Robertson first made the acquaintance of H. Crabb Robinson,[78] with whom a firm friendship subsequently developed, and who, both as a Unitarian and as a keen admirer of Martineau, in whose sermons he found "delight",[79] may very well have stimulated Robertson's interest in Martineau. It is not without significance in this regard, furthermore, that Robinson's *Diary* for 1848 reveals that Robertson read a number of sermons, including some by the Unitarian, Thomas Madge, upon the recommendation of Crabb Robinson.[80] The latter, it may be added, went on to regard Robertson as "the best preacher I ever saw in a pulpit"[81] and described him as understanding "almost every orthodox doctrine in a refined sense such as would shock the mass of ordinary Christians".[82]

There is some ground also for thinking that Robertson was familiar with the writings of Martineau's colleague, J. J. Tayler. It has already been seen that Crabb Robinson found Robertson's and Tayler's views on inspiration and prophecy to be identical,[83] and in a letter to the same writer, Lady Byron, who was a great friend of Robertson, records, after referring to Tayler, that "a book of his was a great treasure to my daughter on her death bed".[84] In view of the intimacy between Robertson and Lady Byron, and the fact that he "attended the dying bed of her daughter",[85] it is not unlikely that the book— probably *Christian Aspects of Faith and Duty*[86]—was read, either upon the recommendation, or else with the approval, of Robertson.

Theodore Parker was another Unitarian not without some influence upon Robertson,[87] and so was Emerson.[88] Far more important, however, was Channing, concerning whom and Robertson the latter's biographer writes as follows: "He revered and spoke of Dr. Channing as one of the noblest and truest Christians of America. He was deeply indebted to his writings. He read them carefully, and borrowed from them largely. He spoke with indignation against those who would un-Christianize Channing, because in words he denied the coequal Divinity of Christ with the Father. He said, if the deepest love is the deepest worship no man adored Christ more sincerely than Channing."[89] Thus regarding a "religious lady" who was horrified at his reading *Channing's Memoirs* Robertson wrote: "I told her that if she and I ever got to heaven, we would find Dr. Channing revolving round the central light in an orbit immeasurably nearer than ours, almost invisible to us, and lost in a blaze of light";[90] and in an unpublished sermon declared: "For what is it to adore Christ? To call Him God; and say Lord, Lord? No. Adoration is the mightiest love the soul can give—call it by what name you will. Many a Unitarian, as Channing, has adored, calling it only admiration; and many an orthodox Christian calling Christ God with most accurate theology, has given him only a cool intellectual homage."[91] To his own nephew he wrote: "Pray do not give up 'Channing's Life', nor read it by starts, but consecutively, and, if possible, regularly at a fixed hour."[92] "It was", as J. W. Chadwick affirmed, "not Channing's approximation to an orthodox Christology that delighted F. W. Robertson, but his enthusiasm for the moral worth of Jesus."[93]

Channing's influence upon Robertson, moreover, was not confined to the more specifically religious aspect of his work but affected also his attitude to social problems. Channing was deeply concerned with the education and advancement of the labouring classes, and Robertson had a similar interest, which was fostered by his reading of Channing's lectures. His address to working men at Hurstpierpoint was largely inspired by Channing's *Essay on the Elevation of the Working Classes*;[94] and Brooke Herford has stated that it was Channing's lecture on *Self Culture* whose "impulse set F. W. Robertson to his noble work among the working classes at Brighton".[95]

Robertson died at the early age of thirty-seven, and after only thirteen years in the ministry. During that short period his theology underwent considerable change. Whether, had he lived longer, and continued to drink from the same theological sources, he might have become, like Brooke later, a Unitarian is an open question.

The ramifications of Channing's and Martineau's influence upon Broad Churchmen in general it is impossible to trace in detail, but of the fact of such influence there can be no question.

Writing of Channing a century after his birth Charles T. Brooks stated: "He is preached in pulpits where he could not have preached in his lifetime,"[96] and went on to quote Sydney Smith—a Broad Churchman, if ever there was one[97]—who at the conclusion of a Sunday sermon declared, "Do not imagine that this sermon is mine,—I cannot do such things,—it is by an American, Dr. Channing."[98] In a letter to Lady Grey in 1844 Smith wrote, "I think Channing an admirable writer"[99] and went on to joke about his use of one of Channing's sermons at St. Paul's—probably the one to which Brooks referred.

Dean Stanley, in conversation with James Martineau,

declared that "when he was in America he believed he never preached a single sermon without mentioning the honoured name of Channing",[100] and, at the centenary celebrations of the birth of Channing, in an address composed by him for that occasion, but read for him by Martineau, Stanley declared that "not once only, nor in one generation only, Channing's sermons have been preached in the pulpit of our own Metropolitan Cathedral".[101] Commenting on this address *The Methodist* rightly stated that its object "seemed to be to show how near Channing's standpoint was to that of the Broad Churchmen",[102] for, after comparing Channing with Thomas Arnold, Stanley placed him in a list composed largely of such names as Falkland, Tillotson, F. W. Robertson and Dean Milman.

The sales of Channing's sermons were enormous.[103] Just how many Broad Churchmen were influenced by them, or, in fact, made use of them in writing their sermons "without affording the opportunity for a critical congregation to detect . . . the source from whence they proceeded"[104] it is impossible to determine. But the use of Unitarian sermons did not go entirely undetected, and in justification of their return to the Church of England some Unitarians cited, among other reasons, the fact that "its preachers deliver such excellent sermons—sometimes taken from well-known Unitarian divines".[105]

Martineau's influence was also very extensive, Hoatson, indeed, giving it as his opinion that "no preacher and teacher of the last century did more to inspire the modern pulpit".[106] It was the reading of Martineau's *Endeavours* along with Maurice's *Kingdom of Christ* that led to the beginning of J. W. Colenso's change from an Evangelical to a more liberal position.[107] In a letter to his fiancée he wrote in 1844, after quoting a passage from Martineau's sermon "Eden and Gethsemane":[108] "But I must not go on in this way filling up my sheet with other men's words, however good and precious, though, in truth, I have few thoughts of my own, now that I have so little exercise of mind in writing and meditation, with which to supply their place. I have never seen a book—I think I may say—so full of *brilliant* and truthful passages as this little work (not excepting even Maurice—as to the former epithet) I have given you indeed but a most feeble and unworthy idea of him—but hope to bring it with me when I see you next—but—he is James Martineau, the Unitarian!"[109]

Years later, Martineau, who developed, as did other Unitarians,[110] a valued friendship with the Bishop, tried to secure for Colenso the Chair of Old Testament and Hebrew at Manchester New College, London, of which Martineau was Principal at the time. The Bishop was willing to give the matter serious consideration, but Martineau's plan fell through as a result of the decision of the College Committee that it would have been "inconsistent for a College which rested on the principle of perfect intellectual freedom to appoint as one of its Professors a clergyman who was bound by his subscription to the creeds and articles".[111] Martineau was on terms of intimate friendship with a number of other distinguished representatives of the Anglican Broad Church, including Lord Tennyson—who considered Martineau to be the greatest member of the famous "Metaphysical Society"[112]—Professor Jowett, and Dean Stanley. The mention of these latter is not intended to indicate that Martineau had any material influence upon them. All that is claimed is that their contact with him—both through friendship and through the printed page—must have strengthened their existing liberal tendencies. It was contact with men such as these that increased Martineau's desire for a comprehensive church, about which more in a later chapter; and it was contact with men such as Martineau that led Dean Stanley to invite the Unitarian scholar, Dr. G. Vance Smith, to participate in the communion service at Westminster Abbey in connection with the Revision of the New Testament.[113] The measure of Martineau's esteem for Stanley may be gathered from a passage from a letter he wrote after the death of Stanley. "With him", he said, "the greatest *personal* power I have ever known has passed from us. The loss to London in particular is something quite unique."[114] It is not without interest that the last letter penned by Stanley was addressed to James Martineau and written the day before the Dean's death.[115]

With Benjamin Jowett Martineau had a stimulating and much valued friendship. Writing to Miss A. Swanwick in 1879 he says of Jowett: "there is no-one whose intercourse is to me more suggestive of thoughts both new and true than his";[116] and it gave Martineau great pleasure to entertain the Master of Balliol at his home in Scotland and be invited in return to stay with Jowett at Oxford.[117] He "very much admired Jowett's college sermons".[118] The influence in the case of this friendship can hardly have been one-sided, and that it was not so is suggested by the testimony of Miss Elliot, Jowett's fiancée, who observed regarding Jowett's "flirting with the Unitarians" at Bristol that in his theological views he "came very near them" in spite of Jowett's view that "they come so near us".[119] It was at Bristol, it may be added, that Jowett first met Frances Power Cobbe, with whom he became friendly, and whose book, *Broken Lights*,—an assessment of the religious situation in England from a theistic stand-point—he pronounced "extremely good",[120] and which formed the basis of one of his sermons preached in London.[121] "Pray urge her to go on with her books," he wrote to one of her friends, and, though he considered she ought to try to give them a more popular appeal, he made it clear that he was "not speaking of changing her ideas".[122] Dean Stanley was similarly appreciative of her writings, and of her article on "Life after Death" declared, "Your writing on this subject is to me more nearly to the truth —at least more nearly to my hopes and desires—than almost any others which are now floating around us."[123] Colenso wrote: "I heartily thank you for your little books . . . I can say no more than that your words speak to my heart throughout."[124] But for his death a few days beforehand Jowett would have made the official welcome of Manchester College to Oxford at its opening in 1893.[125] At the stone-laying two years earlier it may be added, the opening address to the students of the College was given by another Broad Churchman, John Owen, the Rector of East Anstey, North Devon, an author of several studies of scepticism.[126]

A. H. Craufurd, Martineau's Broad Church biographer,

repeatedly refers to Martineau as "my teacher"; and though he was "conscious of differing from some of his views in many important ways" nevertheless declared: "hardly any other modern teacher has helped me so much as Dr. Martineau has done in the multitudinous difficulties of my intellectual and religious life".[127]

Though most of the influence between Unitarianism and the Anglican Broad Church flowed in the latter direction, the Broad Church was not without influence in Unitarian circles. Something of this has already been seen, but further evidence must be presented, and in the next chapter the effect of the Broad Church ideal in the shape of a comprehensive Church will also be noted.

Henry Solly, the Unitarian minister who became the first secretary of the Working Men's Club and Institute Union in 1862, derived not a little inspiration for his work in this connection from his friendship with F. D. Maurice, who founded the Working Men's College in London in 1854. Solly attended the initial meeting with regard to the founding of the latter College and heard Maurice outline the principles upon which it was to be established.[128] Years later he declared: "I left the meeting with a great light thrown upon more than one problem in which I had long felt the deepest interest."[129]

But Maurice's influence upon Solly also extended to the theological realm. Solly attended Maurice's Bible-class,[130] and for some of the ideas in his *The Doctrine of Atonement* Solly was indebted to Maurice.[131] Of one of Maurice's *Lincoln's Inn Sermons* Solly declared: "I know of nothing that has been, or could have been, either then or at any time, of greater help and comfort to me."[132] Maurice, it may be added, was not unappreciative of Solly's sermons, and it was upon Maurice's advice that Solly sent one of his sermons to Charles Kingsley, who replied: "I have read your sermon with the liveliest pleasure. You are right, utterly right. This is what we want, what the world wants, and is hungering for; and will never rest till it hears in all its fulness. Go on, and God be with—God will be with you."[133] For Solly Maurice was "one of the greatest

Englishmen of this century",[134] and the Unitarian minister was pleased to call himself a "disciple"[135] of the great Anglican. Dean Milman was another Broad Churchman for whom Solly confessed "admiration"—in this case his contributions to Biblical and Ecclesiastical history, and especially to hymnology, being the object of Solly's regard.[136]

L. P. Jacks, later editor of the *Hibbert Journal* and Principal of Manchester College, dated his Unitarianism from the reading of Matthew Arnold's *Literature and Dogma*.[137] Arnold's notion of "a Power-not-ourselves that makes for righteousness" had a profound effect upon his life, forming, in fact, the leading concept in his "first religious experience";[138] and "Arnold's way of treating the Book of Authority as Great Literature and letting your mind 'play freely' round its contents" was a very important factor in establishing Jacks' liberal attitude in matters of religion.[139]

Samuel Greg, the prominent Unitarian layman, could have been speaking for many Unitarians when in 1867 he wrote: "My own sympathies turn more strongly to Dean Stanley—Jowett—and Stopford Brooke just now than to any other teachers. I may not be of their opinions but my nature feels more in harmony with theirs:—and I think that they and their like have more of the life without which the form is *dead*."[140] Mary Carpenter, an equally prominent laywoman, was "*much* delighted" with Colenso and his work,[141] and of F. W. Robertson her biographer declares: "She was powerfully moved by his teachings, and never lost her high appreciation of them."[142] A leading article in the Unitarian periodical, *The Inquirer*, stated in 1860: "the writings of the Broad Churchmen find among no section of the religious community so hearty a sympathy and so widespread a reception as among ourselves".[143]

Quite apart from all this the Broad Church had another effect upon Unitarianism of no small importance—the effect of making Unitarians feel that they were part of a larger whole, which was forward looking and advancing. It gave them confidence to think that men like Colenso and Jowett and Stanley had an outlook similar to themselves. They were not an ecclesiastical back-water, but heralds of a new day and something far bigger than themselves.

This, no doubt, was a partial reason for the absence of any tendency on the part of Unitarian ministers to secede to the Anglican Broad Church, and the research involved in the present study has brought to light only one case of a Unitarian minister becoming an Anglican Broad Church parson.[144] It is interesting to observe, however, that Lord Lyttelton was willing to find a Church of England living for Henry Solly;[145] and that, after congratulating H. W. Crosskey on his appointment as minister of the Church of the Messiah, Birmingham, Charles Voysey, the Broad Church Vicar of Healaugh, wrote to the Unitarian minister—whose "wise and temperate teaching" he wished might spread—in the following terms: "If I regretted anything, I should deplore that your new charge was not a parochial one, in connection with the Church of England; but I live in hopes that there will, before very long, be nothing to prevent your joining our ranks, and occupying our pulpits."[146]

No chapter on the influence between Unitarianism and the Anglican Broad Church would be complete without some reference to Joseph Blanco White, and, in spite of the fact that his immediate influence occurred chronologically rather earlier than some of the more recently cited examples, no example could be more suitable with which to conclude, for Blanco White was both a Broad Churchman and a Unitarian, and his influence was felt by both movements.

Originally a Spanish Roman Catholic priest, Blanco White became an Anglican clergyman in 1814 and spent a year in Oxford, whither he returned in 1826 to remain a member of Oriel College until 1831, when he removed to Ireland to reside with his intimate friend Richard Whately, who in that year took up his appointment as Archbishop of Dublin. To avoid embarrassment for the Archbishop he removed from Dublin in 1835 after his announcement of his having become a Unitarian, and settled in Liverpool, where he became a friend of James Martineau, on whom—and through the latter on the Unitarian movement as a whole—he had the important effect of making belief in miracles no longer an essential requisite of the religious life.

Long before he became an avowed Unitarian, however, Blanco White had entertained doubts regarding the Inspiration of the Bible,[147] the Atonement[148] and the Divinity of Christ;[149] and in a private journal he declared of Christ, as early as 1818: "As I believe that he was a man, *in all things, sin excepted*, like ourselves, I cannot persuade myself that he could be GOD, properly so-called."[150] But as he confessed many years later: "In the year 1818 . . . I arrived at the Unitarian view of Christianity; but the perfect obscurity in which I was living, and the consideration that I had not then published anything, except in Spanish, appeared to me a sufficient ground for not making a public avowal of my conviction."[151]

Blanco White's sphere of influence considerably increased, however, when he became a member of the Oriel Common-room, and it was through his membership of the Noetic circle that his influence on the Anglican Broad Church came about. As an ex-Roman Catholic priest, Blanco White was received by his Oxford associates as an authority on patristic and scholastic theology. On these and kindred subjects he was listened to with a respectful ear; and it is interesting to note, in passing, that it was from Blanco White that Pusey, the future Tractarian leader, learned the use of the Roman breviary.[152] But along with such information—to the beliefs involved in which he was vehemently opposed—he contributed a rationalistic attitude which did much to establish the liberal outlook which characterized the Noetics at Oriel.[153] Both Whately and Hampden, Liddon remarks, were "his pupils", and "Arnold and even Hawkins felt his positive influence, though less directly".[154] "Many years before he became a professed Socinian", Liddon continues, "his eager, remorseless unappeasable dialectic was gnawing away at all that was fundamental in the Christian creed and life. To minds with a bias towards a meagre creed and an easy theory of living, he was a welcome teacher. Whately and Hampden sat at his feet, as he laid down his theories on subjects of which they knew nothing, or pointed out corruptions of Christianity, primitive, Anglican, and even Protestant, no less than Roman, with the confidence that among his hearers no one could answer him."[155] The testimony, too, of J. H. Newman, the future Cardinal, that "the conversation of Mr. Blanco White" led him "to have freer views on the subject of inspiration than were usual in the Church of England at the time"[156] is a further indication of the general effect of the influence of Blanco White.

Of especial interest is the matter of his influence on R. D. Hampden, who in 1832 preached the Bampton Lectures on *The Scholastic Philosophy considered in its relation to Christian Theology.* Here Hampden expounded the then revolutionary view that traditional orthodoxy was not identical with simple Christian belief, but the product of speculation and inference in the light of the philosophy in vogue in a previous age. "The speculative language of these Creeds", he said in reference to the Nicene and Athanasian formularies ". . . was admitted into the Church of England . . . before the period, when the genius of Bacon exposed the emptiness of the system, which the Schools had palmed upon the world as the only instrument for the discovery of all Truth."[157] Scripture recorded the facts, but the dogmas of theology were merely inferences, the work of man, and subject to change. "If this account of the origin and nature of Dogmatic Theology be correct", he declared, "surely those entirely pervert its nature who reason on the Terms of doctrines, as if they were the proper ideas belonging to Religion; or who insist on the interpretation of expressions . . . in a positive sense; without taking into their view, the existing state of theology and philosophy at different periods of Christianity."[158] Though Hampden subsequently affirmed his adherence to the traditional doctrines, the effect of his exercise was to weaken their authority; and for a long time his orthodoxy was under suspicion—a suspicion not diminished, moreover, by Hampden's subsequent admission that "when I look at the reception by the Unitarians of both the Old and New Testament, I cannot, for my part, deny those who acknowledge this basis of Divine facts, the name of Christians".[159] "*Who*, indeed", he added, "is justified in denying the title to anyone who professes to love Christ in sincerity?"[160]

Now though attempts have been made to deny the influence of Blanco White in the Bampton Lectures—and for the obvious reason that he so soon afterwards publicly avowed his Unitarianism—there can be little doubt that he played an important part in their production.[161] For they contain not only the kind of information that Blanco White was so pre-eminently, and so conveniently, able to supply, but they also exhibit essentially the same critical attitude as Blanco White towards the subject. As long ago as 1819 Blanco White had written *Facts and Inferences*, "an argument to prove that Christian salvation does not require belief in Articles",[162] which was fundamentally the same work as his *Observations on Heresy and Orthodoxy*, published in 1835, wherein he maintained that "the whole *patristical* theology, which makes up the greatest part of the Thirty-Nine Articles consists in groundless speculation which could never have obtained currency among Christians without the aid of a false philosophy";[163] and refers to orthodoxy as "acquiescence in a certain collection of abstract deductions from the scriptures as logically true, or properly inferred from the language of scripture".[164] How closely akin Hampden's views were to this needs no demonstration.

Thomas Mozley, moreover, who was resident at Oriel from 1825 to 1832,[165] and well acquainted with the relationship between Hampden and Blanco White, declared that "in the latter part of 1831 and the early part of 1832, these two gentlemen saw a good deal of one another, and that one of them derived from the other material assistance in the way of information, authors to be read, and general insight into the subject".[166] His reference to their meeting one another "almost daily"[167] is corroborated, furthermore, by the testimony of Canon Hinds Howell, Blanco White's pupil during 1831 and 1832, that "for a year together scarcely a day passed without Hampden's coming to consult his learned friend".[168] Hampden himself, moreover, made no claim to complete independence, and in a letter written to Whately in 1835 confessed: "I have certainly tried to think for myself, and have had a fondness for taking up subjects of discussion which appeared to me not to have been fully treated before, because they coincided with my turn of mind, or stimulated my curiosity more than others. At the same time I have not pursued the study with the vanity of an independent thinker. I have always sought every information that I could obtain, whether from books or conversation."[169]

It is true, of course, that before the Bampton Lectures were written, Hampden had published his *Essay on the Philosophical Evidence of Christianity* in 1827, and had contributed the articles on Aristotle and Aristotle's Philosophy in the 7th edition of the *Encyclopaedia Britannica*, which was published from 1830 onwards, as well as an article on Thomas Aquinas in the *Encyclopaedia Metropolitana*. But in view of the foregoing evidence, and the fact that "at the time the Lectures were written there was only one man in Oxford who knew anything about the scholastic philosophy, and that was Blanco White",[170] with whom Hampden had been on terms of close friendship since 1814, there can be little doubt that Blanco White not only guided Hampden in his choice of subject and material, but also—and this is the significant fact for this present study—provided him with the critical bias with which he approached it. Hampden's point of view as expressed in the Lectures is essentially that of Blanco White, though he eschewed taking the final plunge into manifest heresy which the latter expected and himself eventually took. This rationalistic influence Blanco White powerfully exerted on all his friends over a long period. And while Liddon may very well have claimed more than he should when he wrote, in 1893, "Of Blanco White's positive influence, it is not too much to say that he is the real founder of the modern Latitudinarian school in the English Church,"[171] there can be no question that to this secret Unitarian the later Broad Church leaders ultimately owed more than they cared to acknowledge, or perhaps even knew.

CHAPTER 6

The Affinity shown in the Commitment to the Idea of a Broad Church

Besides the similarities which have so far been considered there remains one, viz., the commitment of both groups to the idea of a Broad Church, which has yet to receive attention, and in this connection it will be of added interest to observe the attitude of Broad Churchmen towards the inclusion of Unitarians, and the attitude of the latter towards the National Church.

That the Broad Churchmen were committed to the idea of a comprehensive Church is, of course, indicated by their very name. The term "Broad" Church is but a simplification of the earlier "Latitudinarian"; and the Broad Churchmen were the nineteenth-century representatives of the Latitudinarian school of thought, some of whose characteristics were illustrated in the first chapter. The desire of the Broad Churchmen, in the words of Thomas Arnold—whose *Principles of Church Reform* (1833) was one of the chief Broad Church contributions to the subject —was for "a church thoroughly national, thoroughly united, thoroughly Christian, which should allow great varieties of opinion, and of ceremonies and forms of worship, according to the various knowledge, and habits, and tempers of its members, while it truly held one common faith, and trusted in one common Saviour and worshipped one common God".[1] In his view all Dissenters, apart from Quakers and Roman Catholics, should be brought within the fold of the National Church;[2] and the parish churches should be the centres for all worship, with the alternative times for liturgical and non-liturgical services.[3]

A number of textbooks referring to Arnold credit him with

the view that the Unitarians should be excluded.[4] But this is not entirely correct. His own words on the subject were: "With regard to the Unitarians, it seems to me that in their case an alteration of our present terms of communion would be especially useful. The Unitarian body in England consists of elements the most dissimilar; including many who merely call themselves Unitarians, because the name of unbeliever is not yet thought creditable, and some also who are disgusted with their unchristian associates, but cannot join a church which retains the Athanasian Creed. Every means should be taken to separate these from their unworthy society, that they who are really unbelievers might be known by all the world to be so."[5] And he added later: "Addressing Christ in the language of praise and prayer is an essential part of Christian worship. Every Christian would feel his devotions incomplete if this formed no part of them. This therefore cannot be sacrificed; but we are by no means bound to enquire whether all who pray to Christ entertain exactly the same views of his nature. I believe that Arianism involves in it some very erroneous notions as to the object of religious worship; but if an Arian will join in our worship of Christ, and will call him Lord and God, there is neither wisdom nor charity in insisting that he shall explain what he means by these terms; nor in questioning the strength of his faith in his Saviour, because he makes too great a distinction between the divinity of the Father, and that which he allows to be the attribute of the Son."[6] And when in the postscript to *Principles of Church Reform* he added: "If a man will not let me pray to and praise my Saviour, he destroys the exercise of my faith altogether;—but I am no way injured by his praying to him as a glorified man, while I pray to him as God"[7] Arnold had gone even beyond admitting Arians, for a "glorified man" is definitely less than an Arian Christ. Had they wished to do so, the majority of Unitarians might have qualified for comprehension within the National Church on Arnold's terms.

But it may be asked: Was Arnold a lone figure among Broad Churchmen in desiring to include the Unitarians? The answer is certainly in the negative. Arnold's great pupil, Dean Stanley, as early as 1834 declared of the Unitarians: "They are, I think, excluded from the outward Catholic Church as a body, but their individual members are not from the Communion of Saints";[8] and many years later, as has already been seen, he caused great offence by inviting a Unitarian to partake of the sacraments at Westminster Abbey, which latter, in keeping with Arnold's conception of the function of the parish church, he sought to make a national shrine for the use of all, irrespective of dogmatic creed.[9] Opposed to clerical subscription,[10] Stanley saw the essence of Christianity not in doctrine, but in Christian character.[11] Thus he could not reject out of hand the possibility of a man such as Martineau, at some future date, becoming Archbishop of Canterbury; and stood like the great Unitarian for a "liberal theology", which, "whilst comprehending all the wholesome elements of thought at work within the world, yet holds that the Christian belief is large enough to contain them; which insists, not on the ceremonial, the dogmatic, or the portentous, but on the moral side of religion."[12]

The same insistence on the moral aspect of religion, along with the desire for a perhaps even greater comprehensiveness, was expressed by H. B. Wilson in his contribution to *Essays and Reviews*. The national church, he thought, should concern itself with the "ethical development" of its members. "Speculative doctrines should be left to philosophical schools",[13] and, in the interest of the Church's wider appeal, provision should be made to ensure that "the Church teaching and forms of one age do not traditionally harden, so as to become exclusive barriers in a subsequent one".[14] It is true that Wilson did not specifically mention the Unitarians, but it is difficult to imagine, on these principles, that he could have wished to exclude them, particularly when he declared that "the freedom of opinion which belongs to the English citizen should be conceded to the English Churchman"[15] and that "a national Church need not, historically speaking, be Christian, much less, if it be Christian, need it be tied down to particular forms which have been prevalent at certain times in Christendom".[16]

Similarly, when W. G. Clark, the Vice-Master of Trinity

College, Cambridge, stated in his *True and False Protestantism* (1871) that he "dreamed of a Church which, exacting no formal confession of faith from any of its members, tolerant of differing rituals, admitting the authority of presbyters, elders, and ministers, beside that of the bishops and the priests, should gather into one fold and unite in one common cause all who believe in Christ as the most divinely-gifted messenger of God",[17] he did not specifically mention Unitarians, but the phrase "the most divinely-gifted messenger of God" exactly expressed the Unitarian view of Jesus; and Clark's book received favourable mention in the pages of *The Inquirer*.[18]

Dean Alford, in outlining a scheme for the "union of Christendom", declared, about the same time, that "you cannot bound Christendom by a doctrinal test",[19] and urged that consideration of the latitude of doctrine allowed to Churchmen should "cause any honest man to drop the stone which he had lifted to throw at the Unitarian".[20] So, too, G. H. Curteis, in his *Dissent and its Relation to the Church of England* (1871), after noting, among other things, that "in personal character many Unitarians represent the very highest type of Christian manhood" and that "in ecclesiastical matters their tendency is rather towards the Church of England than away from her",[21] maintained: "It is impossible for any observant man to believe that the separation of the Unitarians from the Church is a fundamental or permanent one."[22] And Canon W. H. Fremantle, after pleading, in 1886, for the recognition of Unitarians as "brother Christians", expressed the viewpoint, not only of Broad Churchmen, but also of Unitarians, when he declared: "The hope cannot be suppressed that a relationship which begins with trustfulness will go on to a deeper sense of unity in spirit and in principle, and lead eventually to a common expression of our union in faith and life."[23]

But how far were the Unitarians committed to the idea of a Broad Church? As was seen in the first chapter, the English Presbyterian forbears of the nineteenth-century Unitarians stood for a broad comprehensiveness tolerant of differing shades of theological opinion. With this went also a certain sympathy for the Established Church, for the ejected ministers of 1662 were "unwilling nonconformists" and for a number of years still hopeful of comprehension within the national church. Thus it may be said that from its English Presbyterian past Unitarianism had already inherited the concept of itself as a Broad Church, and possessed certain Anglican sympathies, which were reinforced by the influence of Theophilus Lindsey, whose use of a modified form of the Anglican *Book of Common Prayer* was a constant reminder to Unitarians of the existence of the Anglican Church and of their link with it through a basically similar pattern of worship.

At the beginning of the nineteenth century, after the influx of a number of converts who, in reaction against their orthodox past, tended to emphasize the theological tenets of Unitarianism in a propagandist and denominationalistic manner, there was some danger that this aspect of Unitarianism might be lost.[25] But the older influence was still powerful, and even such an ardent denominationalist and controversial theologian as Thomas Belsham was sufficiently influenced by the older spirit of comprehension to dream, in 1820, of a national church wherein there should be "no doctrinal test but the profession that Jesus Christ is a teacher come from God, that he died and rose again, and that the Scriptures of the Old and New Testaments contain everything necessary to faith and practice".[26] And he remarked also, though on another occasion: "I think my church ought to be established, but as it cannot be, I would rather the Anglican Church should be maintained."[27]

But if there was a danger, early in the century, that the influence of denominationalistically-minded converts was going to lead to Unitarianism's losing sight of the principle of broad comprehensiveness, something was soon to happen which was to re-establish very firmly commitment to this principle. It is unnecessary to go into the precise details since the facts may be easily found elsewhere,[28] but between the years 1817 and 1844 the right of Unitarian tenure of a chapel at Wolverhampton and of the benefits of the Lady Hewley Charity was challenged on the ground that the original endowments were made by orthodox Dissenters, and that therefore the Unitarians had no right to them. In a series of court actions case after case went against the Unitarians, and their tenure of many other chapels inherited from their English Presbyterian past was placed in jeopardy. Only by the passing of the Dissenters' Chapels Act in 1844, which provided that, when trust deeds did not specify the doctrines to be maintained, twenty-five years' tenure was sufficient to make existing doctrinal usage legitimate, was the danger averted.

During the long period within which the litigation was in process the Unitarians laid great stress on the fact that the trust deeds of their chapels were "open"[29]—which, they argued, provided for slow theological change—and also that the transition from orthodox to Unitarian belief had been gradual and with no conscious break in continuity. This experience led to a strong re-emphasis on the part of Unitarians, particularly as a result of the leadership of such men as James Martineau and J. J. Tayler, on the essentially comprehensive character of their Church.[30] "Though for individual believers", said Martineau in a pamphlet significantly entitled *Church Life? Or Sect Life?*, "definite theological conviction is important to the spiritual life; and for simultaneous fellow-worshippers a corresponding theological sympathy is indispensable, yet it is wrong for permanent Churches to fix their standard of belief, and commit their religious life to the hazards of a specific type of doctrine."[31] There was always a possibility of change, and only a church free from doctrinal prescriptions could cope with that change. For this reason he disliked, since in his view it was a doctrinal term, even the use of the word "Unitarian" as the name of the church to which he belonged. "If anyone, being a Unitarian", he said, "shrinks, on fitting occasion, from plainly calling himself so, he is a sneak and a coward."[32] And he added: "If, being of our catholic communion, he calls his chapel or its congregation Unitarian, he is a traitor to his spiritual ancestry, and a deserter to the camp of its persecutors."[33] For Martineau a sect was made by a "temporary concurrence in theological opinion" that "embodies itself in a creed", whereas it was "conscious sameness of spiritual relations"[34] that made a church; and he was anxious "only till better days" that Unitarians should "keep open and unexclusive some little corner in the Church meant to be Universal".[35]

It was in the interest of hastening the arrival of these "better days" that Martineau, along with J. J. Tayler and other Unitarian ministers, formed in 1867 the "Free Christian Union"[36] which aimed at a "catholic"[37] union on the basis of spiritual rather than dogmatic affinity. The union drew support from a number of Nonconformists, but apart from the Unitarians, the main sympathy for its objects came from Broad Churchmen,[38] who included Henry Sidgwick, the Cambridge philosopher, who became its Vice-President, and C. Kegan Paul.[39] And it is significant that J. J. Tayler, in his *A Catholic Church the Want of our Time* (1867), which was designed to explain the purpose of the Union, declared, with an obvious reference to Broad Churchmen: "Within the last five-and-twenty years . . . the most valuable contributions to a large-hearted and generous theology, and the most fearless encounter of the complicated problems it involves, have proceeded, not from the sectarian ranks, but from men belonging to the National Church."[40] It was, in fact, the following "very truth of truths" from Thomas Arnold, viz., "Christian unity and perfection of Christ's Church are independent of theological articles of opinion; consisting in a certain moral state and moral and religious affections"[41] that in part inspired the Free Christian Union's statement of its aims.

Although through lack of support, and in particular that occasioned by the death of J. J. Tayler, the Free Christian Union came to an end in 1870,[42] Martineau's active concern for its essential ideal remained undiminished, and in 1885 he became involved with R. Bosworth Smith, the Rev. Sir G. W. Cox and other Broad Church Anglicans in the affairs of the "National Church Reform Union",[43] which urged that the basis of the Anglican Church should be "as widened as to include, as far as possible, the entire Christian life and thought of the nation".[44] "For nearly fifty years", Martineau wrote in 1885 to Bosworth Smith, "I have been a most unwilling Nonconformist; compelled to be so by inability to accept the Theology of the Anglican formularies; but believing in a fundamental unity of religious sentiment in the English people, attaching great importance to its National expression, and longing for the time when the ban of exile may be removed which excludes so large a multitude at present shut out from Church Communion."[45] "Mere personal banishment, however", he continued, "has no effect in diminishing my historical reverence and social affections for the most venerable and beneficent of all English institutions; the gates of which I would still defend from assault, even though her fellowship were to be denied for ever to such as I am."[46] It was in this connection that Martineau published his *The National Church as a Federal Union*[47] (1887), whose essential features appeared in the draft of a Bill which it was abortively hoped would be presented to Parliament.[48] Martineau proposed that "any Christian denomination at present counted as Dissenting shall be co-ordinated with the Episcopalian as another branch of the Church of England, on showing its hold on the English religious life by a history of one hundred years and a magnitude of two hundred congregations, and also its adequate provision for education and character in its ministers".[49] The Episcopalian Church should be disestablished, but retain all the endowments which were indisputably her own, i.e., those made subsequently to 1662, when by the Act of Uniformity she was marked off from the remainder of the religious life of the nation; while all the Churches fulfilling the previously mentioned conditions should receive "proportionate participation"[50] in the endowments made prior to 1662, which stand "in an impartial relation to the religious growths of later times and must be taken as conferred upon the entire Christendom of England".[51] The resulting confederation of communions would constitute an enlarged "Church of England" and have their collective representation in a "National Church Assembly".[52] Although, unlike Arnold, Martineau did not envisage the parish churches as being the centres for all worship, it is difficult to see how, if a "proportionate participation" was to be achieved, some sharing of the older church buildings could have been entirely avoided, and, in fact, his view that all communions should "on adequate occasions"[53] have use of the cathedrals is not dissimilar to Arnold's conception with regard to the parish churches. Indeed, it is not impossible that Martineau had some of the previously quoted passages from Arnold in mind—his devotion to Arnold was "almost unreserved"[54]—when, about this time, he published his essay, "A Way Out of the Trinitarian Controversy"[55] (1886), wherein he sought to show that the Unitarian worship of the Father was in essentials the same as the Trinitarian's worship of the Son. Both conceptions of God involved the same attributes. "The faith professed in 'the Son' ", he said, ". . . is identical, under change of name, with the Unitarian's worship of Him who dwelt in Christ. He who is the Son in the one creed is the Father in the other; and the two are agreed, not indeed by any means *throughout*, but in that which constitutes the pith and kernel of both faiths."[56] "Let the advocates of each", he said, "compare them together from this point of view, with mind open, not to words only, but to the real thoughts they contain, and with temper sensitive to sympathy rather than to divergency, and there is hope that we may yet all come into the unity of faith, and true knowledge of the Son of God."[57]

CHAPTER 7

Conclusion: The Nature of the Affinity

The substantial affinity between Unitarianism and the Anglican Broad Church having now been shown, it remains to consider a number of questions regarding the nature of that affinity. At the levels of higher criticism and theology there can be no doubt that the affinity that existed was the product of a rationalistic, yet sensitive, approach to religion. For the Unitarians and Broad Churchmen the intellectual aspect of religion was of particular importance; and they were especially concerned that their religion should be reasonable, and able to meet the strains and stresses produced by contemporary thought. It was, in fact, this rationalistic tendency that distinguished the Broad Churchmen from their fellow Anglicans, and the Unitarians, as "rational Dissenters",[1] from the rest of Nonconformity. And for this reason, apart from the inevitable kinship which the Broad Churchmen naturally shared with their fellow Anglicans, any other affinities which any other church groups in England might share with either the Broad Churchmen or the Unitarians—for example, the affinity of Baptists with Unitarians as fellow Nonconformists—were of an altogether negligible character. Indeed, The Inquirer could say: "All secessions from our ranks are in the direction of the National Church—seldom, if ever, towards other Nonconformist denominations,"[2] just as Lyulph Stanley could truly remark: "The Broad Church party ... if it was in kinship with any other Church besides the Church of England, was in kinship with Unitarianism."[3]

But even at the less important level of affinity in liturgical practice the emphasis on rationality was still present, at least on the Unitarian side.[4] For although the Unitarian use of liturgies largely based on the *Book of Common Prayer* was, to a considerable extent, the incidental result of the influence of Theophilus Lindsey's Latitudinarian past, the readiness of Unitarians to employ such a mode of worship was the consequence of a desire to be orderly, dignified, restrained, and, as the frequent revisions of their liturgies show, *reasonable*. But, even without those revisions, there was a sufficiency of the previously mentioned qualities in the Anglican service, when conducted by a Broad Churchman, to ensure that "Unitarians living at a distance from their place of worship", did, as *The Inquirer* put it, "almost invariably show a natural predilection for the well-ordered and dignified Church service in preference to the barren and unpoetical worship of the Independent or Methodist meeting house".[5]

Unitarians, in fact, never entirely lost the feeling that their English Presbyterian forefathers possessed, viz., that they ought to be part of the National Church, and assume a place of importance at the centre of things—a feeling which was reinforced by the fact that perhaps the majority of Unitarians belonged to the increasingly powerful middle class.[6] Indeed, there can be little doubt that, besides more worthy motives, consciousness of social position was not a negligible factor behind the Unitarian use of a liturgy and Gothic architecture,[7] which, like the frequent use of the word "church", as opposed to "chapel", to designate their new buildings, was an "assertion of equality with the Establishment".[8] But even here the motive of reasonableness, which is a particularly middle-class characteristic, may be discerned, for it was not so much their superiority to the, in their eyes, more plebeian character of the generality of Nonconformity—for the latter, too, possessed a social elite—as their strong distaste for the emotionalism and the general absence of stress on reason, which appeared to characterize much of Nonconformity—and, to many of the latter, Unitarians were "cold"—that they wished to emphasize. And there can be little doubt that whatever the status the Anglican Church possessed, the Unitarians would not have tried to emulate its ways of worship and its decorum, but for the spectacle of Broad Church leaders within it, who embodied so supremely their religious—and middle class—ideal of reasonableness. Nor, for that matter, is it possible to believe that the Broad Churchmen themselves would have remained within the Anglican fold had they not felt it possible to bring their own faith into a rational relationship with the problems of their times.

But was this rational approach, which constituted the essential bond between the Unitarians and Broad Churchmen, the result of entirely separate developments? There can be no question that many Anglicans, for example, Thomas Arnold and A. P. Stanley, became Broad Churchmen purely as a result of their own insights and proclivities; and it is impossible to believe that there would have been no Broad Church but for the existence of Unitarianism—indeed, something more like the reverse is true, for it is dubious whether Unitarianism would have been as widespread as it was, but for the influence of Dr. Samuel Clarke's *Scripture-doctrine of the Trinity*, which was productive of much of the eighteenth-century Arianism which developed further into the Unitarianism of the nineteenth century, and which, as a Latitudinarian work, may be classed as an early form of "Broad Church" influence. However, in the period more immediately under discussion the balance was to some extent redressed, for it is certainly true to say that Unitarian thought and writings acted as a powerful catalyst in the production, and encouragement of Broad Churchmen; and the influence of Channing and Martineau went wide and deep, both F. W. Robertson and Stopford Brooke showing that there might well have been fewer, or, at the very least, less ardent, Broad Churchmen, but for the existence of their writings.

But this emphasis on the rationalistic tendency of the Unitarians and Broad Churchmen must not lead to a failure to recognize the fact of another, and not insignificant, affinity between them, viz., that existing by reason of their moral and religious sensitivity. In spite of the frequent accusation that their religion was barren, cold, and either consisted of, or led to, a "rationalism, pure and simple",[9] they were often acutely sensitive, possessing as, for example, did Martineau, along with the intellect of the rationalist, the vibrant heart of the saint; and the opposition of a Colenso or a Crosskey to the doctrine of Everlasting Punishment proceeded as much from his sense of moral and religious indignation as from his intellectual disagreement with the dogma. And it was from the marriage of this sensitivity, which was able to penetrate behind the doctrines that divide to the essential spiritual core of religion in which all religious men share, with the rationality which claimed for all men the right to think differently, according to their best insights, within a Christian framework, and saw the futility and irrationality of good men engaged in theological warfare, that the Broad Church ideal was born.

But it was an ideal that was destined never to be realized. As the trial resulting from the publication of *Essays and Reviews* clearly showed, the Broad Churchmen were stretching the capacity of their Church to dangerous limits. The further radicalism of Unitarianism could never have been tolerated. As laymen Unitarians could, and some did, join the Established Church. But for the Unitarian minister there could be no way in, even to become a Broad Churchman, without the surrender of the liberty, which, more than anything else, except his belief in God, he held dear. Only the most drastic changes in the National Church could have secured his entrance, and it would have meant the end of the Anglican Church as it has existed for centuries. For the sake of the admission of two to three hundred Unitarian ministers, of high intellectual and spiritual calibre though they might be, to a Church consisting of some 18,000 clergy,[10] would it have been worth it? Both from the Anglican and from the Unitarian points of view it is difficult to believe that it would.

Notes

In the following notes *D.N.B.* signifies *Dictionary of National Biography*.

CHAPTER 1

1. F. L. Cross, *Oxford Dictionary of the Christian Church*, 1957, p. 199.

2. The "Unitarian Church" did not technically come into existence until 1928, when the British and Foreign Unitarian Association (1825) and the National Conference of Unitarian, Liberal Christian, Free Christian, Presbyterian and other Non-Subscribing or Kindred Congregations (1881) amalgamated to form the General Assembly of Unitarian and Free Christian Churches. But provided that the term "Unitarian Church" is not taken to mean a formally organized body, it is a convenient term to use in the present context. The British and Foreign Unitarian Association was formed in 1825, by the amalgamation of three previously existing associations, the earliest of which was brought into formal existence in 1791.

3. Unitarian congregations existed, of course, before this date, but Lindsey's chapel in Essex Street, London, was the first to be specifically called "Unitarian".

4. The popular use of the term "Broad Church" probably dates from October 1853, when in the *Edinburgh Review* W. J. Conybeare in an unsigned article entitled "Church Parties", p. 273 ff., set forth the characteristics of this party and stated, p. 330 ff., that it had been called "Moderate, Catholic, or Broad Church, by its friends; Latitudinarian or Indifferent by its enemies". See C. R. Saunders, *Coleridge and the Broad Church Movement*, 1942, p. 7.

5. The term "Noetics" was derived from the Greek νοητικός, "pertaining to the intellect", and used of the group of early nineteenth-century thinkers who were members of the Senior Common Room of Oriel College, Oxford.

6. The term "English Presbyterian," coined in the seventeenth century, was revived in the 1830's by the English Unitarians who were defending themselves against the orthodox Dissenting attack, chiefly Congregational, on their possession of the Lady Hewley Trust, etc. (for details regarding the latter see Chapter 6); and in 1834 they formed an "English Presbyterian Association" for purposes of defence. They did not claim to be "Presbyterians", without the epithet "English", as this would confound them with the Scottish type, both in Scotland and in London, but claimed (not without justification) to be, and to be descended from, a specially English type. In 1662 the great majority of the ejected clergy were called Presbyterian, which meant that they be-

longed to the middle party of the Puritans, who had wanted a reformed state-church with a parochial system, as distinct from the Independents and sectaries who emphasized the gathered church. It is this group of Presbyterians and their descendants who are here referred to as "English Presbyterians"; and it is convenient to do this, as do other writers, to avoid their confusion with those Presbyterians who remained loyal to Calvinism. A number of Unitarian chapels still retain the name "Presbyterian". The English Presbyterians should not be confused with members of the "Presbyterian Church of England", which was formed in 1876, and which is orthodox in its beliefs.

For further details see: T. Falconer, *The History, Opinions, and Present Legal Position of the English Presbyterians*, 1834; J. Wilson, *An Historical Inquiry concerning the Principles, Opinions and Usages of the English Presbyterians*, 1834; and the appendix to *The Christian Reformer*, 1834, entitled "The English Presbyterian".

The story of *The English Presbyterians* is told in a book of that title, by C. G. Bolam, J. Goring, H. L. Short, and R. Thomas, which was published in 1968, after this note was originally written.

7. O. M. Griffiths, *Religion and Learning—a Study in English Presbyterian Thought from the Bartholomew Ejections (1662) to the Foundation of the Unitarian Movement*—Introduction, 1935.

8. From a funeral oration following the death of his father, 1703. Quoted by J. E. Carpenter, *James Martineau*, 1905, p. 206.

9. The Trinitarian Controversy was begun by Stephen Nye's publication of the *Brief History of the Unitarians or Socinians* in 1687. See E. M. Wilbur, *A History of Unitarianism—in Transylvania, England, and America*, 1952, pp. 218 ff. This controversy was, of course, largely an Anglican affair, but it did not go unnoticed by Dissenters, and some Presbyterians were involved. For the latter's involvement, see Robert Wallace, *Antitrinitarian Biography*, I, 1850, p. 253.

10. F. E. Mineka, *The Dissidence of Dissent*, 1944, p. 12. It is true that the provisions of the Toleration Act involved subscription to the doctrinal Articles of the Church of England by Dissenting ministers, and thus the doctrines to be preached in the chapels were, at least theoretically, controlled, yet it is noteworthy that P. Henry, for example, was unhappy about such subscription, as there were points in the Articles which "without a candid construction would somewhat scruple me" (see *Dictionary of National Biography*, XXVI, p. 126), and that the "openness" of the trust deeds was fully in accordance with his scruples.

It is possible that some nineteenth-century Unitarians over-emphasized the significance of these "open" trusts (see Chapter 6), but the freedom which the English Presbyterians tolerated shows that there was more significance in this than some subsequent writers have allowed. Note how Nathaniel Carter, in a will dated 1722, in which he bequeathed property for the benefit of two congregations at Filby and Great Yarmouth (both of which became Unitarian), expressly declared, as quoted in *The Christian Reformer*, 1836, p. 883: "And because no person, who designs the glory of God, the prosperity of his Church, and the support of his interest in the world in ages after his decease, can foresee the changes and revolutions that may arrive, and which might oblige him to alter and change the particular method by which he proposeth such ends should be promoted; my great and general instruction to these my Trustees is this: that the purposes of sincere Piety and Charity, according to the best light of their consciences, and agreeable to the directions of the Word of God, may be industriously and faithfully served to the utmost of their ability by this entrustment, leaving with them this short and serious memento, GOD SEES."

11. E. Calamy, *Nonconformist's Memorial*, III, 2nd ed., 1803, p. 155.

12. E. Calamy, *An Historical Account of My Own Life*, I, 1829, p. 342.

13. Moses Lowman, *Occasional Papers*, II, No. 1, 1716, p. 23. This passage is interestingly quoted in the constitution of the Free Christian Union—in Free Christian Union Papers in Dr. Williams's Library, 14 Gordon Square, London, W.C.1. See references to the Free Christian Union in Chapter 6.

Strictly speaking Lowman was an Independent, but his sympathies were with the English Presbyterians whose attitude is exemplified in his words. He sought intellectual fellowship with Presbyterian ministers rather than with his denominational brethren, and it is probably because of this that he has sometimes been referred to as a Presbyterian, as by W. Turner, *Lives of Eminent Unitarians*, 1840, p. 267. It was a Presbyterian divine, Dr. Chandler, who preached at his funeral and who was responsible for the posthumous publication of some of his work. *Occasional Papers* was a Presbyterian periodical published from 1716 to 1719.

14. Quoted by J. Drummond and C. B. Upton, *Life and Letters of James Martineau*, I, 1902, p. 12.

15. R. Baxter, *Autobiography of Richard Baxter*, ed. by J. M. Lloyd Thomas, 1925, p. 136. The term "catholic" as used by the English Presbyterians meant comprehension and mutual toleration.

16. E. M. Wilbur, op. cit., p. 181.

17. E. M. Wilbur, op. cit., p. 175.

18. E. M. Wilbur, loc. cit. Cf. H. Hallam, *Introduction to the Literature of Europe*, I, 4th ed., 1854, p. 558—Acontius (Aconcio) "instances, among doctrines which he does not reckon fundamental, those of the real presence and of the Trinity; and in general, such as are not either expressed in Scripture, or deducible from it by unequivocal reasoning", and he adds "Aconcio was not improbably an Arian".

19. J. Tulloch, *Rational Theology and Christian Philosophy in England in the 17th Century*, I, 2nd ed., 1874, p. 168.

20. J. Tulloch, op. cit., I, p. 163. Cf. John Aubrey, who says in *Brief Lives, Chiefly of Contemporaries set down by John Aubrey, between the years 1669 and 1696*, edited by A. Clark, 1898, p. 150, of Falkland, "He was the first Socinian in England".

21. J. Hales, *Works*, I, 1765, pp. 126 ff. Quoted by J. H. Elson, *John Hales of Eton*, 1948, p. 126. E. M. Wilbur, in *A History of Unitarianism in Transylvania, England, and America*, 1952, p. 182, writing of Hales, says, "His ideas of tolerance were undoubtedly derived from Socinian writings", and he adds, "His reputation as a scholar and a preacher gave him much influence in making the Church more hospitable to reason and tolerance—

thus paving the way toward Socinianism and the later Unitarianism."
Interestingly enough, in the seventeenth century, and later, two books by
Socinian writers were mistakenly attributed to Hales' authorship—see
J. H. Elson, *John Hales of Eton*, 1948, pp. 118 and 173.

22. E. M. Wilbur, op. cit., pp. 183–4.

23. In a letter to a friend on the subject of Arianism quoted by P. Des
Maizeaux in his *An Historical and Critical Account of the Life and Writings of
William Chillingworth*, 1725, p. 56, Chillingworth maintains that "the doc-
trine of Arius is either a truth, or, at least, no damnable heresy".

24. E. Stillingfleet, *Irenicum*, 1662, Chapter II, p. 108.

25. E. Stillingfleet, op. cit., p. 107.

26. G. G. Perry, *History of the English Church*, II, 1887, p. 545. Later, in a
letter dated 23 October 1694, Tillotson wrote of the Athanasian Creed, "I
wish we were well rid of it." The letter is quoted in full by Robert Wallace,
op. cit., pp. 274–5.

27. John Hunt, in an article entitled "The Bishops and the Revision of
the Bible" in the *Contemporary Review*, April 1871. H. R. Fox Bourne in the
Life of John Locke, I, 1876, remarks, p. 311, that Firmin's house "was a
famous resort of the latitudinarian churchmen of Charles the Second's
time". So, too, R. V. Holt remarks in *The Unitarian Contribution to Social
Progress in England*, 1938, p. 285, "Tillotson entrusted Firmin with the choice
of special preachers." On the latter point see also Alexander Gordon, *Heads
of English Unitarian History*, 1895, pp. 23–4.

28. J. E. Carpenter, *James Martineau*, 1905, p. 205.

29. R. Baxter, *Autobiography of Richard Baxter*, ed. J. M. Lloyd Thomas,
1925, p. 139.

30. J. Humfrey, *Mediocria or the Middle Way between Protestant and Papist*.
Letter appended, p. 61—Quoted by O. M. Griffiths, *Religion and Learning*,
1935, p. 108.

31. Peirce, a Londoner, had been a member of Stepney Meeting, a
Congregational church, and is hence sometimes referred to, as by Carpenter, op. cit., p. 207, and Gordon, op. cit., p. 33, as a Congregationalist. For
a reference to Peirce's Presbyterian views see W. Turner, *Lives of Eminent
Unitarians*, 1840, pp. 102–3.

32. The three main Dissenting bodies, viz., the Presbyterians, Congregationalists and Baptists. Immediately after the passing of the Toleration Act,
the Presbyterians and Congregationalists, in particular, had tried to act in
concert with each other in the common interest of Dissent. The union,
however, did not long continue.

33. J. E. Carpenter, *James Martineau*, 1905, pp. 207–8. This should not be
taken, of course, to mean that the English Presbyterians voted on this issue
as a body. However, most of them voted against subscription, and they
formed a majority among the non-subscribers. As time went on non-
subscribers of other denominations gravitated towards the English Presbyterians while the subscribers among the Presbyterians tended to move
towards the Congregationalists.

34. Quoted by V. D. Davies, *A History of Manchester College*, 1932, p. 39.

35. W. Chillingworth, *Works*, 1742 ed., p. 204.

36. Quoted by J. H. Overton and F. Relton, *The English Church 1714–1800*, 1906, p. 30.

37. F. E. Mineka, *The Dissidence of Dissent*, 1944, p. 16. Cf. A. H. Hore, *The Church in England from William II to Victoria*, II, 1886, p. 27, who interestingly refers to the signatories as "Latitudinarian and Socinian Clergy".

38. G. G. Perry, *History of the English Church*, III, 1887, p. 103. All three wrote against subscription. Thus Law published anonymously his *Considerations on the Propriety of requiring subscription to Articles of Faith* in 1774 (*D.N.B.*, XXXII, p. 216); Paley in the same year published, also anonymously, his *A Defence of the Considerations of the Propriety of requiring a subscription to Articles of Faith* (*D.N.B.*, XLIII, p. 106); and Watson wrote his *A Letter by a Christian Whig* anonymously in 1772 (Watson, *Anecdotes of the Life of Richard Watson*, I, 2nd ed., 1818, pp. 69–70—also *D.N.B.*, LX, p. 25).

39. E. M. Wilbur, op. cit., p. 278. Paley refused to sign because he "could not afford to Keep a conscience". See A. H. Hore, op. cit., p. 27, footnote, also *D.N.B.*, XLIII, p. 102.

40. Duncan Coomer, *English Dissent under the Early Hanovarians*, 1946, pp. 78–9. Cf. H. S. Skeats and C. S. Miall, *History of the Free Churches of England 1688–1891*, 1891, p. 248, who, writing from an orthodox viewpoint and in reference to the effects of the Salters' Hall Conference, remark: "In less than half a century the doctrines of the great founders of Presbyterianism could scarcely be heard from any Presbyterian pulpit in England."

41. E. M. Wilbur, op. cit., pp. 237–8.

42. E. M. Wilbur, op. cit., p. 239.

43. E. M. Wilbur, op. cit., p. 240. See C. J. Abbey and J. H. Overton, *English Church in the Eighteenth Century*, 2nd ed., 1887, pp. 204 ff.

44. J. H. Colligan, *The Arian Movement in England*, 1913, p. 30.

45. G. G. Perry, *History of the English Church*, III, 1887, pp. 29–30.

46. For the more traditional "through Jesus Christ our Lord" Hoadly frequently substitutes such expressions as "in his Name and as his Disciple". See *Plain Account of the Nature and End of the Lord's Supper*, ed. 1735, p. 218. See especially the Preface to the Prayers, pp. 175 ff., for Hoadly's more general position.

47. Quoted by J. H. Overton and F. Relton, *The English Church 1714–1800*, 1906, p. 27, with the comment, "It was not a groundless alarm."

48. Quoted by Theophilus Lindsey, *Historical View of the State of Unitarian Doctrine and Worship from the Reformation to our own Times*, 1783, p. 136. Also quoted in abbreviated form by A. H. Hore, *The Church in England from William III to Victoria*, II, 1886, footnote, p. 15. The orthodoxy of Matthew Hutton, Herring's successor, was also dubious. See A. H. Hore, *The Church in England from William III to Victoria*, II, p. 20; also A. Gordon, *Addresses Biographical and Historical*, 1922, p. 248.

Dr. John Jortin, it may be added, was Archdeacon of London, and was a Latitudinarian. At a fairly early stage in his ecclesiastical career he gave up the use of the Athanasian Creed.

49. A. H. Hore, *The Church in England from William III to Victoria*, II, 1886, p. 20. Cf. also Wilbur, *History of Unitarianism in Transylvania, England, and America*, 1952, p. 273.

50. A. H. Hore, *The Church in England from William III to Victoria*, II, 1886, p. 33. Also, *Monthly Repository*, XIII, 1818, p. 292, footnote.

51. Compare p. 313 (and footnotes) of Law's *Considerations on the Theory of Religion*, new edition, 1820, with pp. 2–3, and footnotes on p. 3 of Law's *Reflections on the Life and Character of Christ*, 1760 ed. The *Reflections on the Life and Character of Christ*, it should be added, formed part of the later editions of Law's *Considerations on the Theory of Religion*.

52. "I must desire your acceptance of a new Cumberland edition of my Theory, purged of some ancient prejudices relative to pre-existence, etc." The letter, which is dated "Cambridge, September 23rd, 1783", is reproduced by Thomas Belsham in a footnote on p. 121 of his *Memoirs of the Late Reverend Theophilus Lindsey*, 2nd ed., 1820. (The letter, of course (September, 1783), was written before the final edition, to which it refers, was actually published, the date of publication being 1784.) The fact that "to Arianism Lindsey was never drawn" (A. Gordon, *Addresses Biographical and Historical*, 1922, p. 248) and that "he was a confirmed believer in the humanity of our Lord" (A. Gordon, loc. cit.) *may* indicate that Law drew attention to the alteration because he had now passed beyond an Arian to a humanitarian position. This evidence, of course, is not proof, but is nevertheless suggestive of such an interpretation.

53. R. N. Stromberg is incorrect when on p. 48 of his *Religious Liberalism in 18th Century England*, 1954, he gives the date as 1754.

54. "*A Frenchman in England 1784*"—being the *Mélanges sur l'Angleterre* of *François de la Rochefoucauld*—edited by Jean Marchand and translated with notes by S. C. Roberts, 1933, p. 92. La Rochefoucauld's statement is rather sweeping, but doubtless contains some truth.

55. The statement occurs in a Latin speech before the University—"In disputationibus theologicis ab usu vocabulorum quae in sacro codice non reperiuntur, qualia sunt οὐσία, ὁμοουσία, ὁμοιουσία, τριας, peccatum originale, sacramentum, satisfactio, quantum potui abstinere, religio mihi fuit." See Richard Watson, *Anecdotes of the Life of Richard Watson, Bishop of Llandaff*, I, 2nd ed., 1818, p. 299.

56. "Ne verbis ἀγράφοις ad dogmata etiam ἀγραφα propaganda utamur." R. Watson, op. cit., I, p. 299.

57. R. Watson, *Miscellaneous Tracts on Religious, Political and Agricultural Subjects*, II, 1815, p. 108.

The tract, which is entitled "The Expediency of Revising the Liturgy and Articles", was first published, anonymously, in 1790; and the authorship was acknowledged in 1815.

58. Thomas de Quincey, *Works*, II, entitled *Recollections of the Lakes and the Lake Poets*, 1862, p. 3. Leslie Stephen in his *History of English Thought in the Eighteenth Century*, I, 1876, p. 456, also refers to this passage, though he refers to De Quincey as "an extremely loose reporter of facts". Possibly Stephen's hesitation, however, concerns only the remainder of De Quincey's statement, which continues: "he ridiculed the miracles of the New Testament, which he professed to explain as so many chemical tricks, or cases of legerdemain".

59. C. J. Abbey and J. H. Overton, *The English Church in the Eighteenth*

Century, I, 1st ed., 1878, p. 515, footnote. Both Rundle and Hare were members of the "society for Promoting Primitive Christianity" (1715–17) founded by the heretical William Whiston. In his *Memoirs of the Life and Writings of Mr. William Whiston*, written by himself, Whiston records, p. 233, 2nd ed., 1753, his surprise at Rundle's determination to take Holy Orders, and refers also, p. 105, to "Dr. Hare's scepticism in religion". Hare's *Difficulties and Discouragements which attend the Study of the Scriptures in the way of Private Judgement*, 1714, was censured by Convocation. See Augustus J. G. Hare in *D.N.B.*, XXIV, p. 366.

60. See the article entitled "Archdeacon Paley a Unitarian" in *The Christian Life*, 11 July 1891, pp. 334 ff., and the subsequent articles on pp. 370 ff. and 408. The evidence there presented it should be stated, however, is insufficient, in spite of the title, to do more than suggest that Paley was probably an Arian. He was certainly not a humanitarian, as the title might suggest.

Leslie Stephen in *English Thought in the 18th Century*, I, 1876, p. 421, remarks: "The theology of Paley, Hey and Watson is only nominally Trinitarian and their orthodoxy may, with little want of charity, be imputed to the fact that they attached too little importance to their dogmas to care for a collision with the Thirty-nine articles." See also note 39 on this latter point.

61. John Hey, *Lectures in Divinity*, I, 3rd ed., 1841, p. 367.

Hey's conception of the importance of the doctrine of the Trinity may be judged from the following: "It would be an improvement if *forms* could be invented in which Socinians could join: in which, while we addressed ourselves to the Holy Ghost, they could use the same words, and address themselves to *God*, independently of the Holy Trinity, while we took some expressions as *plain*, implying a *real* person, they should take them as rhetorical, or as instances of the prosopopaeia, or metonymy" (ibid., p. 649). The italics are Hey's own.

62. Frend, it is interesting to note, was largely responsible for Coleridge's adoption of Unitarianism. See J. Gillman, *The Life of S. T. Coleridge*, I, 1838, p. 317; J. Dykes Campbell, *Samuel Taylor Coleridge*, 2nd ed., 1896, p. 25.

63. Alexander Gordon, *Heads of English Unitarian History*, 1895, pp. 31–2.

64. F. E. Mineka, op. cit., p. 13.

65. F. E. Mineka, loc. cit.

66. F. E. Mineka, loc. cit. The quotation from Locke, which is given more fully by Mineka, comes from Locke's "Essay concerning Human Understanding", Book I, chapter 4, section 12. See J. Locke, *Philosophical Works*, I, 1877, p. 191.

67. H. McLachlan, *The Religious Opinions of Milton, Locke and Newton*, 1941, p. 107. See also E. M. Wilbur, op. cit., p. 232, who, writing as a Unitarian, says ". . . it was Locke's (anonymous) 'Reasonableness of Christianity as delivered in Scriptures' (1695) that gave especial stimulus to our movement".

68. *Christian Reformer*, 1851, p. 615. For a good account of the episode see J. E. Carpenter, *James Martineau*, 1905, pp. 359–64, especially pp. 362–4.

69. A. Gordon, *Heads of English Unitarian History*, 1895, p. 32.

70. For Peirce see H. McLachlan, *The Unitarian Movement in the Religious Life of England*, 1934, p. 26; for John Taylor, op. cit., pp. 27–8; for Belsham, op. cit, p. 41. See also J. J. Tayler, *A Retrospect of the Religious Life of England*, 2nd ed., 1876, pp. 240–1.

71. H. McLachlan, *The Unitarian Movement in the Religious Life of England*, 1934, p. 22. F. E. Mineka, op. cit., p. 14. *The Unitarian Tracts*, published between 1691–1703, were the work of Anglican writers.

72. J. H. Colligan, *The Arian Movement in England*, 1913, p. 46.

73. E. M. Wilbur, op. cit., p. 254.

74. E. M. Wilbur, op. cit., p. 253. J. Hallet's son secretly corresponded with Whiston, loc. cit.

75. E. M. Wilbur, op. cit., p. 254. Also A. Gordon, *Addresses Biographical and Historical*, 1922, pp. 127–8. H. McLachlan, op. cit., p. 16.

76. H. McLachlan, *The Unitarian Movement in the Religious Life of England*, 1934, p. 227.

77. *Memorable Unitarians*, 1906, p. 67. (No name of author or editor given.)

78. T. Belsham, *Memoirs of the Late Reverend Theophilus Lindsey*, 1820, p. 75.

79. A. E. Peaston, *The Prayer Book Reform Movement in the 18th Century*, 1940, p. 59.

80. G. E. Evans, *Antiquarian Notes*, III, 1904, part 27, pp. 101–2.

81. *Monthly Repository*, XIII, 1818, p. 291, footnote. Also T. Belsham, *Memoirs of the Late Reverend Theophilus Lindsey*, 2nd ed., 1820, p. 342, footnote.

82. J. Tillotson, *Sermons*, 1728, p. 71.

83. G. W. Meadley, *Memoirs of William Paley*, 1810, p. 310. The fifth commentator was Locke, whose influence with regard to Unitarianism has already been alluded to. Both Peirce and Hallet were important in the matter of the Salters' Hall Controversy. Benson (1699–1762) is described by Grosart in *D.N.B.*, IV, p. 256, as "undoubtedly a Socinian, a fact which explains the neglect that attended his works after his death". McLachlan, however, comments in *The Unitarian Movement in the Religious Life of England*, 1934, p. 27, "He was certainly Socinian in his view of the Atonement, but not otherwise, though a well-founded suspicion of his heterodoxy doubtless led to the result mentioned by his biographer."

84. Leslie Stephen, *History of English Thought in the Eighteenth Century*, I, 1876, p. 414. Lardner, it may be mentioned, began as an Independent, but subsequently became a Presbyterian.

85. The letter is reproduced in T. Belsham, *Memoirs of the Late Reverend Theophilus Lindsey*, 2nd ed., 1820, p. 342, footnote. Law, incidentally, was the most liberal of the subscribers.

86. The letter, which is dated "Cambridge, September 23rd, 1783", is reproduced in a footnote on p. 121 of T. Belsham, op. cit.

87. Cf. C. P. S. Clarke, *Short History of the Christian Church*, 3rd ed., 3rd impression, 1956, p. 483. "A. P. Stanley and Benjamin Jowett . . . kept up the Noetic tradition, but by 1850 the Noetics were beginning to be known as Broad Churchmen."

88. F. W. Cornish in *History of the English Church in the Nineteenth Century*, I, 1910, p. 186, says that the Broad Church school "may be divided both

intellectually and chronologically into two sections, the philosophical and the critical or historical. The first may be said to begin with Coleridge and end with Maurice . . . ; and the second derived their impulse from the sceptical inquiries of German theologians into the history of religion, and produced in England the literature of which Arnold was one of the harbingers, though he did not extend his inquiries into forbidden regions, and Milman, whose bold inductions roused the antipathy and disgust of Newman and the Tractarians".

As to the use of the term "philosophical", V. F. Storr in *The Development of English Theology in the 19th Century*, 1913, p. 338, remarks of the Coleridgean and Mauricean school: ". . . the movement may be called philosophical, because the ideas which inspired it were in large part derived from German philosophy, and because all the writers named were specially interested in determining the value and significance of the deepest utterances and aspirations of the human consciousness. It had philosophical depth, even if it did not embody itself in a philosophical system".

F. P. Cobbe in her *Broken Lights: an Inquiry into the Present Condition and Future Prospects of Religious Faith*, 1864, uses the terms "First Broad Church" and "Second Broad Church" to denote the two sections and gives the following succinct statement of the main differences: "The First Broad Church maintains that the doctrines of the Bible and the Church can be perfectly harmonized with the results of modern thought by a new but legitimate exegesis of the Bible and interpretation of Church formulae. The Second Broad Church seems prepared to admit that, in many cases, they can only be harmonized by the sacrifice of Biblical infallibility. The First Broad Church has recourse, to harmonize them, to various logical processes, but principally . . . of diverting the student, at all difficult points, from criticism to edification. The Second Broad Church uses no ambiguity, but frankly avows that when the Bible contradicts Science, the Bible must be in error. The First Broad Church maintains that the Inspiration of the Bible differs in *kind* as well as in *degree* from that of other books. The Second Broad Church appears to hold that it differs in degree but *not* in kind," (pp. 73-4.)

89. E. M. Wilbur, op. cit., pp. 368–70. See also R. V. Holt, *The Unitarian Contribution to Social Progress in England*, 1938, p. 342.

CHAPTER 2

1. Referring to the period 1825–6, E. B. Pusey (H. P. Liddon, *Life of Edward Bouverie Pusey*, I, 1893, p. 72) said: "At that time only two persons in Oxford were said to know German." See also V. F. Storr, *The Development of English Theology, 1800–1860*, 1913, p. 177; and L. E. Elliott-Binns, *English Thought, 1860–1900*, 1956, p. 26: "Before 1860, though German work on the classics was fairly well known, few English theologians were at all familiar with what was being done on their special subject." T. Belsham writing in 1819 said (*Memoirs of T. Belsham* by J. Williams, 1833, p. 704): "I know but two persons in this country who are disciples of the German theology."

Notes

2. V. F. Storr, *The Development of English Theology: 1800–1860*, 1913, p. 177.

3. Davidson's heresy was expressed in the second volume of T. H. Horne's *On Introduction to the Critical Study and Knowledge of the Holy Scriptures*, which volume he edited in 1856. His heresy consisted in his surrender of the Mosaic authorship of the Pentateuch, and his view that the inspiration of the Bible did not include the infallibility of its statements regarding science, history, etc. In spite of the mild character of his views, he was bitterly attacked in contemporary periodicals. *The Inquirer*, however, as might be expected, spoke, in a review of the book, on 20 December 1856, p. 811, of Davidson's "singular good sense", and welcomed the volume. Davidson's book was given only moderate praise as a critical work by T. K. Cheyne in *Founders of Old Testament Criticism*, 1893. W. B. Glover, in *Evangelical Nonconformity and Higher Criticism in the 19th Century*, 1954, p. 257, somewhat harshly ventures to "seriously question whether his influence did much to hasten the acceptance of higher criticism in England".

In his *An Introduction to the New Testament*, 1848, Davidson took note of critical views, but his conclusions were all in line with traditional opinions. His earlier *Lectures on Biblical Criticism*, 1839, which was republished in 1852 as *A Treatise on Biblical Criticism*, was wholly concerned with matters of textual criticism.

Some idea of the very conservative attitude of both Nonconformists and Churchmen in matters of Biblical study may be gathered from a perusal of T. H. Horne's *An Introduction to the Critical Study and Knowledge of the Holy Scriptures*, which, in spite of its title, can hardly be called "critical" at all. The book may be said to represent the general position of both Churchmen and Nonconformists, not only by reason of its wide use (see Preface to the second edition, 1821), and its many editions (it was first published in 1818, and there were many subsequent editions continuing well into the second half of the nineteenth century), but also because Horne, who became an Anglican clergyman in 1819, carried out the main work in the production of the book while still a Methodist. For reference to Horne's work on the book while a Methodist, see T. H. Horne, *Reminiscences Personal and Bibliographical of Thomas Hartwell Horne*, 1862, p. 20.

In the notes which follow, reference to Horne's work, a standard reference book of the period, will occasionally be made for comparison with the writings discussed.

W. Robertson Smith's work falls outside the scope of the statement regarding the conservative tendency of English Nonconformist Biblical study in the first sixty or so years of the century: Smith's work was done in Scotland, and was carried out in a period later than that under immediate discussion. Even so, it is worth noting that Smith was dismissed from his chair at Aberdeen in 1881 for undermining belief in the inspiration of the Bible.

See further J. E. Carpenter, *The Bible in the Nineteenth Century*, 1903; T. K. Cheyne, *Founders of Old Testament Criticism*, 1893; W. B. Glover, *Evangelical Nonconformists and Higher Criticism in the Nineteenth Century*, 1954. For a general reference to the conservatism of Nonconformity, see V. F. Storr, op. cit., pp. 455 ff.

4. L. E. Elliott-Binns, *Religion in the Victorian Era*, 1936, p. 146.

Bishop Herbert Marsh translated into English Michaelis' *Introduction to the New Testament*, 1793–1801, along with his own "hypothesis" on the origin of the first three Gospels, which was much attacked; and, writing in 1860, Mark Pattison, in *Essays and Reviews*, 5th ed., 1861, p. 262, tartly commented: "That investigation introduced by a bishop and professor of divinity, has scarcely yet obtained a footing in the English Church. But it is excluded, not from a conviction of its barrenness, but from a fear that it might prove too fertile in results."

E. B. Pusey, who later became eminent as a Tractarian leader, published in 1828 his *An Historical Enquiry into the Probable Causes of the Rationalist Character lately predominant in the Theology of Germany*, and a sequel in 1830, but the books excited disapproval and were withdrawn. Pusey's later position may be seen from his *Daniel the Prophet*, 1864, in which he defended the traditional authorship.

5. L. E. Elliott-Binns, op. cit., p. 147.

6. From a letter written in 1858 by Benjamin Jowett to Dean Stanley. See E. Abbott and L. Campbell, *Life and Letters of Benjamin Jowett*, I, 1897, p. 275.

7. Printed in 1795, and quoted in the "Memoir", pp. xix and xx, Volume I of T. Kenrick's *Exposition of the Historical Writings of the New Testament*, published posthumously in 1807.

8. C. Wellbeloved, *Three Letters addressed to the Ven. and Rev. Francis Wrangham, M.A., Archdeacon of Cleveland in his reply to his remarks on Unitarianism and Unitarians*, 2nd ed., 1823, p. 51.

9. From the Preface, p. vii, Kenrick, op. cit. That doctrinal considerations sometimes played a part in this matter is, of course, not impossible, and is suggested by H. Solly, himself a Unitarian, in *These Eighty Years*, I, 1893, p. 101, when, in reference to Unitarians of the school of Priestley and Belsham, he remarked that they "implicitly accepted the divine authority of nearly the whole of the New Testament, explaining away those passages which distinctly assert the opposite view, with a most curious and, as it seemed to me, perverse ingenuity".

10. Until Oxford and Cambridge universities were opened to Dissenters in 1871, it was customary for some of the latter's theological students to study on the Continent. See L. E. Elliott-Binns, *English Thought*, 1956, p. 26. Among Unitarians who thus studied abroad may be mentioned J. J. Tayler (Göttingen), P. H. Wicksteed (Leiden), G. Vance Smith, James Martineau.

11. E. Evanson, *The Dissonance of the Four Generally Received Evangelists*, Preface, 2nd ed., 1805, pp. ix, x; p. 22, etc.

12. E. Evanson, op. cit., p. 273.

13. E. Evanson, op. cit., p. 284.

14. E. Evanson, op. cit., pp. 307 ff.

15. H. McLachlan, *The Unitarian Movement in the Religious Life of England*, 1934, p. 50.

16. T. Belsham, *A Summary View of the Evidence and Practical Importance of the Christian Revelation*, 2nd ed., 1809, pp. 35–6.

17. *The Annual Review and History of Literature*, VII, 1808 (but printed 1809), p. 293.

Notes

18. A. Gordon, *Addresses Biographical and Historical*, 1922, p. 304.

19. John Williams, *Memoirs of the late Reverend Thomas Belsham*, 1833, pp. 704–5.

20. J. Williams, op. cit., p. 705.

21. T. Belsham, *The Epistles of Paul the Apostle Translated with an Exposition, and Notes*, I, 1822, Preliminary Dissertation, Sectio II, p. xxviii.

22. J. Priestley, *Notes on all the Books of Scripture, for the use of the Pulpit, and Private Families*, I, 1803, p. 1.

23. T. Belsham, *A Summary View of the Evidence and Practical Importance of the Christian Revelation*, 2nd ed., 1809, p. 116.

24. T. Belsham, *Reflections Upon the History of Creation in the Book of Genesis. A Discourse delivered at Warrington*, 19 August 1821, p. 26.

25. T. Belsham, op. cit., p. 29.

26. *Essays and Reviews*, 5th ed., 1861, p. 338.

27. C. C. Hennell, *Inquiry Concerning the Origin of Christianity*, preface, 1838. See also Strauss' prefatory note in J. W. Cross, *George Eliot's Life*, I, ed. 1885, p. 101.

28. C. C. Hennell, op. cit., preface, p. iv.

29. C. C. Hennell, op. cit., p. 80.

30. C. C. Hennell, op. cit., pp. 74–5.

31. C. C. Hennell, op. cit., p. 87. In this, of course, he was accepting the judgment of Augustine.

32. C. C. Hennell, loc. cit.

33. C. C. Hennell, op. cit., p. 90.

34. C. C. Hennell, op. cit., p. 93 and footnote.

35. C. C. Hennell, op. cit., p. 97.

36. C. C. Hennell, op. cit., p. 104.

37. C. C. Hennell, op. cit., p. 106.

38. C. C. Hennell, op. cit., p. 109.

39. C. C. Hennell, op. cit., pp. 108–9.

40. C. C. Hennell, op. cit., p. 228.

41. C. C. Hennell, op. cit., pp. 260 ff.

42. C. C. Hennell, op. cit., p. 244.

43. C. C. Hennell, op. cit., preface, p. vii.

44. C. C. Hennell, op. cit., pp. 35 ff.

45. L. E. Elliott-Binns, *Religion in the Victorian Era*, 1936, p. 151.

46. F. W. Newman, *The Hebrew Monarchy*, 2nd ed., 1853, preface, p. viii.

47. F. W. Newman, op. cit., p. 295.

48. F. W. Newman, op. cit., p. 300.

49. F. W. Newman, loc. cit.

50. F. W. Newman, op. cit., p. 47.

51. Contrast T. H. Horne, *Introduction to the Critical Study and Knowledge of the Bible*, IV, ed. 1856, p. 411: "Matthew is generally supposed to have written first of all the Evangelists." Note also the following remarks of S. Davidson regarding Mark's Gospel in his *An Introduction to the New Testament*, I, 1848, p. 162: "It is impossible to ascertain the precise time when the Gospel was written. Two extremes, however, should be avoided—the idea that it is the most ancient of all the Gospels, as Weisse, Wilke, and B. Bauer

135

maintain; and the idea of Fritzche, who conjectures that it was written last. Both opinions seem to us manifestly untenable, the truth lying between them."

52. *Prospective Review*, 1850, pp. 65 ff.

53. Both Eichhorn and Marsh were exponents of the hypothesis of an original written Gospel and of numerous subsequent revisions. Both theories were extremely complicated. Andrews Norton believed that "the Gospels remain essentially the same as they were originally composed" and "that they have been ascribed to their true authors". See A. Norton, *The Evidence of the Genuineness of the Gospels*, I, 2nd ed., 1847, p. 11.

54. *Prospective Review*, 1850, pp. 61–2.

55. Contrast the viewpoint expressed in the following passage found on pp. 564–5 of T. H. Horne's *An Introduction to the Critical Study and Knowledge of the Holy Scriptures*, II, 9th ed., 1846: "Although the sacred writers, being divinely inspired, were necessarily exempted from error in the important truths which they were commissioned to reveal to mankind, yet it is not to be concealed that, on comparing Scripture with itself, some detached passages are to be found, which *appear* to be contradictory; and these have been a favourite topic of cavil with the enemies of Christianity from Spinosa (sic) down to Voltaire, and the opposers of Divine Revelation in our own days who have copied their objections. . . . Wherever one text of Scriptures seems to contradict another, we should, by a serious consideration of them, endeavour to discover their harmony."

56. W. R. Greg, *The Creed of Christendom*, 1851, pp. 8–9.

57. W. R. Greg, op. cit., p. 38.

58. W. R. Greg, op. cit., p. 42.

59. W. R. Greg, op. cit., p. 43.

60. W. R. Greg, op. cit., p. 57.

61. W. R. Greg, op. cit., p. 58.

62. W. R. Greg, loc. cit.

63. W. R. Greg, op. cit., p. 60. Contrast S. Davidson's words, five years later, on p. 934 of T. H. Horne's *An Introduction to the Critical Study and Knowledge of the Holy Scriptures*, II, 1856: "In whatever light we regard the prophetic book before us, the difficulties of accounting for its origin in the Maccabean period are infinitely greater than any which lie against the Daniel-authorship." And Davidson, it should be added, was felt to be "advanced" and rather dangerous in his critical views.

64. W. R. Greg, op. cit., p. 80.

65. W. R. Greg, op. cit., p. 83.

66. W. R. Greg, op. cit., p. 86.

67. W. R. Greg, op. cit., p. 87.

68. W. R. Greg, op. cit., pp. 88 ff.

69. J. Morley, *Critical Miscellanies*, III, 1886, pp. 242–3.

70. E. Higginson, *The Spirit of the Bible*, I, 1853, p. 3.

71. E. Higginson, loc. cit.

72. For example, as against Hennell, he accepts, op. cit., II, p. 85, "fully and frankly, the miraculous in Christianity as its very basis". But see the discussion of Higginson's views in Chapter 3 of this book.

73. E. Higginson, op. cit., pp. 88 ff.
74. E. Higginson, op. cit., p. 71.
75. E. Higginson, op. cit., p. 72.
76. E. Higginson, op. cit., p. 75.
77. E. Higginson, op. cit., p. 377.
78. E. Higginson, op. cit., p. 393.
79. E. Higginson, op. cit., p. 404. Here Higginson quotes from the article by Samuel Sharpe in *The Christian Reformer*, 1851, p. 480. Sharpe, it may be added, was a keen lay Unitarian Bibilical scholar, and in 1865 published a *Revised Translation of the Bible as a Whole*.
80. E. Higginson, op. cit., p. 442. Contrast S. Davidson's rejection of the non-Isaiah authorship of these chapters three years later on pp. 855 ff. of T. H. Horne's *An Introduction to the Critical Study and Knowledge of the Holy Scriptures*, II, 1856. Davidson, as previously observed, was regarded as having rather dangerous and advanced views!
81. E. Higginson, op. cit., p. 496.
82. E. Higginson, op. cit., pp. 508 ff. Contrast the views of S. Davidson expressed in the quotation in note 63.
83. E. Higginson, *The Spirit of the Bible*, II, 1853, p. 294.
84. E. Higginson, op. cit., p. 306, footnote.
85. E. Higginson, op. cit., p. 330.
86. E. Higginson, op. cit., pp. 498–9.
87. G. V. Smith, *The Prophecies relating to Nineveh and the Assyrians*, 1857, pp. 252 ff.
88. G. V. Smith, op. cit., p. 76.
89. See J. E. Carpenter, *The Bible in the Nineteenth Century*, 1903, p. 395, who refers to Tayler's having "opened the serious discussion of the whole Johannine question to English readers in 1867" by the publication of this book. Observe also that J. J. Tayler is the first name to be mentioned in the list of "critical" English works on the Johannine question by P. W. Schmiedel in his concluding note to "John, the Son of Zebedee" in *Encyclo-paedia Biblica*, II, 1901, column 2562.
   In the 10th edition of T. H. Horne, op. cit., IV, 1856, p. 464, Tregelles, who had the task of bringing the volume up to date, makes a very brief reference to attacks on the traditional authorship and dismisses them as follows: "The importance of these modern theories does not consist in their *ingenuity*, nor in their learning (such as it is) with which they are supported, but simply in their *mischief*."
90. J. J. Tayler, *An Attempt to ascertain the Character of the Fourth Gospel*, 1867, pp. 6–7.
91. J. J. Tayler, op. cit., p. 14.
92. J. J. Tayler, op. cit., p. 144.
93. J. J. Tayler, op. cit., p. 90 and pp. 146–7.
94. J. J. Tayler, op. cit., pp. 150–1.
95. J. J. Tayler, op. cit., pp. 155–6.
96. W. B. Glover, *Evangelical Nonconformity and Higher Criticism in the Nineteenth Century*, 1954, p. 43.
97. *The British Weekly*, 12 August 1887, p. 225. This was doubtless a

reference to Russell Martineau, J. Martineau's son, who was recommended for the post of Lecturer in Hebrew at Manchester New College, London, by Ewald. For a favourable mention of him see T. K. Cheyne, *Founders of Old Testament Criticism*, 1893, p. 211. See T. K. Cheyne, op. cit., pp. 195–6, also for the following comment: "And though contact with German thought began the regeneration of English theology long before 1862, yet neither Hare, nor Arnold, nor Jowett, nor even Stanley, could (for want of Hebrew scholarship and other things) be the predestined champion of reform in the study of the Old Testament."

98. W. B. Glover, *Evangelical Nonconformity and Higher Criticism in the Nineteenth Century*, 1954, p. 110.

99. W. B. Glover, op. cit., p. 44.

100. See L. E. Elliott-Binns, *Religion in the Victorian Era*, 1936, p. 148.

101. W. B. Glover, op. cit., p. 48.

102. O. Pfleiderer, *The Development of Theology in Germany since Kant, and its Progress in Great Britain since 1825*, 1890, p. 388: "For the *Essays and Reviews* contain nothing that had not already been thought and said from the days of Whately and Arnold. . . ."

103. Oriel College, Oxford, was, so to speak, the "headquarters" of the liberal movement in theology in the Anglican Church in the early nineteenth century. For a very brief account of the "Oriel School" see E. C. Moore, *An Outline of the History of Christian Thought since Kant*, 2nd Impression, 1947, pp. 199 ff.

104. J. Davison, *Nature of Prophecy*, 1st ed., 1824, pp. 51–2.

105. J. Davison, op. cit., p. 15.

106. J. Davison, op. cit., p. 118.

107. J. Davison, op. cit., p. 52.

108. J. Davison, op. cit., p. 60.

109. See V. F. Storr, *The Development of English Theology*, 1913, p. 110: "The Noetic spirit of inquiry and historical research was active in two men, Thirlwall and Milman, who though they were not members of the Oriel group, may fairly be classed with it."

110. R. Whately, *Essays on some of the Difficulties in the Writings of St. Paul*, 1828, p. 32.

111. R. Whately, op. cit., p. 36.

112. R. Whately, op. cit., p. 36.

113. R. Whately, op. cit., p. 196.

114. R. Whately, op. cit., p. 222.

115. R. Whately, op. cit., pp. 120–1.

116. R. Whately, op. cit., p. 47.

117. Henry Solly, *These Eighty Years*, II, 1893, p. 81.

118. H. H. Milman, *History of the Jews*, I, 2nd ed., 1830, p. 90.

119. H. H. Milman, op. cit., p. 312.

120. H. H. Milman, op. cit., p. 313.

121. "The Late Dean of St. Paul's" by A. P. Stanley in *MacMillan's Magazine*, January 1869, p. 179.

122. A. P. Stanley, *Life of Arnold*, I, 8th ed., 1858, p. 231.

123. T. Arnold, *Essay on the Right Interpretation and Understanding of Scripture*, 1831, pp. 446 ff.

124. T. Arnold, op. cit., p. 475.

125. T. Arnold, op. cit., p. 477.

126. T. Arnold, op. cit., pp. 481–2.

127. T. Arnold, op. cit., p. 479. Arnold wrote: "I cannot but express my deep regret at the general neglect of the study of Hebrew in this country; and, especially, that it is neither required of candidates for ordination, nor as a qualification for degrees in theology at the Universities."

128. A. P. Stanley, *Life of Arnold*, I, 8th ed., 1858, p. 231.

129. R. J. Campbell, *Thomas Arnold*, 1927, p. 189.

130. Thomas Arnold, *Two Sermons on the Interpretation of Prophecy*, 1839, preface, p. i.

131. A. P. Stanley, *Life of Arnold*, II, 1858, pp. 164–5. Contrast T. H. Horne, op. cit., IV, 1846, p. 206: "Although the name of Daniel is not prefixed to his book, the many passages in which he speaks in the first person sufficiently prove that he was the author." Contrast also E. B. Pusey's defence of the traditional authorship in *Daniel the Prophet*, 1864.

132. W. R. Greg, *The Creed of Christendom*, 1851, p. 24.

133. E. Abbott and L. Campbell, *Life and Letters of Benjamin Jowett*, I, 1897, p. 142.

134. B. Jowett, *The Epistles of St. Paul to the Thessalonians, Galatians, and Romans, with Critical Notes and Dissertations*, I, 2nd ed., 1859, pp. 417–8.

135. B. Jowett, "On the Interpretation of Scripture" in *Essays and Reviews*, 5th ed., 1861, p. 338.

136. A. P. Stanley, *The Epistles of St. Paul to the Corinthians, with Critical Notes and Dissertations*, II, 1855, pp. 311 ff.

137. *Essays and Reviews*, 5th ed., 1861, p. 340.

138. *Essays and Reviews*, loc. cit.

139. *Essays and Reviews*, pp. 340–1.

140. *Essays and Reviews*, p. 367.

141. *Essays and Reviews*, pp. 358–9.

142. *The Inquirer*, 7 July 1860, p. 565.

143. Charles Beard, "Essays and Reviews—The Broad Church", in *The Christian Reformer*, Number CXC, Volume 16, October 1860, p. 598.

144. For an account of the trial and related events see F. W. Cornish, *The English Church in the Nineteenth Century*, part II, 1910, pp. 249 ff.

145. J. W. Colenso, *The Pentateuch and the Book of Joshua Critically Examined*, part I, 1862, p. 8.

146. A brief summary of the most interesting critical conclusions of Colenso in regard to the Old Testament may be found on p. vii of the preface of G. W. Cox, *Life of J. W. Colenso*, I, 1888.

147. F. P. Cobbe, *Broken Lights*, 1864, p. 114.

148. Goblet D'Alviella, *The Contemporary Evolution of Religious Thought in England, America and India*, 1885, p. 91.

Notes

CHAPTER 3

1. F. W. Robertson, *Sermons*, 4th series, new ed., 1882, p. 298.

2. For Unitarian contributions see, for example: C. Beard, *Outlines of Christian Doctrine*, 1859, Chapter 2; W. R. Greg, *Creed of Christendom*, 1851, Chapters 1 and 2; C. Higginson, *Spirit of the Bible*, I, 1853, Chapter 5; J. Martineau, *Rationale of Religious Enquiry*, 1836, Chapter 1; J. Martineau, *Seat of Authority in Religion*, I, 4th ed., 1898, Chapter 4, pp. 114 ff.

For Broad Church contributions, see: T. Arnold, *The Christian Life, its course, its hindrances, its helps*, 1841, pp. 486 ff.; B. Jowett, *Essays and Reviews*, 5th ed., 1861, pp. 344 ff.; C. Thirlwall, in the Introduction, pp. xi ff. to Schleiermacher's *Critical Essay on the Gospel of Luke*, 1825; R. Whately, *Essays on Some Difficulties in the Writings of St. Paul*, 1828, pp. 43 ff.; R. Williams, *Rational Godliness*, 1855, pp. 286 ff.; F. W. Robertson contemplated writing a treatise on the subject. See Stopford Brooke, *Life and Letters of F. W. Robertson*, II, 1891, p. 136.

3. T. Belsham, *Reflections upon the History of Creation in the Book of Genesis. A Discourse delivered at Warrington*, 19 August 1821, p. 26: "If the history of creation in the first chapter of Genesis be inspired, then all the discoveries of Kepler and Galileo, of Copernicus and Newton, are false . . . which is impossible."

4. J. Martineau, *Rationale of Religious Enquiry*, 4th ed., 1853, p. 11.

5. J. Martineau, op. cit., p. 17.

6. C. C. Hennell, *Inquiry concerning the Origin of Christianity*, 1838, preface, p. iv.

7. W. R. Greg, *The Creed of Christendom*, 1851, pp. 26–7.

8. W. R. Greg, op. cit., p. 27.

9. S. T. Coleridge, *Confessions of an Inquiring Spirit*, edited by H. N. Coleridge, 4th ed., 1863, p. 45.

10. W. R. Greg, op. cit., p. 29.

11. E. Higginson, *The Spirit of the Bible*, I, 1853, p. 29.

12. C. Beard, *Outlines of Christian Doctrine*, 1859, p. 48.

13. C. Thirlwall, in the Introduction, p. xi, to Schleiermacher's *Critical Essay on the Gospel of Luke*, 1825.

14. C. Thirlwall, op. cit., p. xii.

15. C. Thirlwall, op. cit., p. xix. In spite of the vagueness of this definition, it is not, however, in disagreement with some of the clearer definitions quoted later.

16. A. P. Stanley, *Life and Correspondence of Thomas Arnold*, I, 8th ed., 1858, p. 178. From a letter, undated, by B. Price.

17. W. R. Greg, op. cit., p. 23.

18. W. R. Greg, op. cit., Preface, pp. viii–ix.

19. W. R. Greg, op. cit., p. 22

20. T. Arnold, *Christian Life, its course, its hindrances, and its helps*, 1841, p. 488.

21. T. Arnold, loc. cit.

22. W. R. Greg, op. cit., pp. 26–7.

23. Here quoted from J. Martineau, "Five Points of Christian Faith" in *Studies in Christianity*, 1858, p. 189, but originally appearing in *The Christian Teacher*, III, 1841.

24. J. Martineau, *The Seat of Authority in Religion*, 4th ed., 1898, p. 308.

25. J. Martineau, loc. cit.

26. J. J. Tayler, *Two Lectures; being the Introduction to a Course on the Early History of Christianity*, 1857, p. vi of the "Advertisement".

27. J. J. Tayler, op. cit., p. 17. Note also Dr. T. Sadler, "The Unitarian of London between Forty and Fifty Years Ago", *The Christian Reformer*, III, 1887, p. 27: "That word 'inspiration' is no longer confined so much as it used to be to the great teachers of old, but is applied also to ourselves, as expressing the secret of all our spiritual understanding, and of all the higher and holier moods and aspirations of our own minds."

28. Stopford A. Brooke, *Life and Letters of Frederick W. Robertson*, I, new ed., 1891, p. 135.

29. Stopford A. Brooke, op. cit., p. 136. Note also that H. C. Robinson, in the *Diary, Reminiscences, and Correspondence of Henry Crabb Robinson*, III, ed. T. Sadler, 1869, p. 392, observed of Robertson: "His definition of inspiration and prophecy is precisely such as is contained in the *Prospective Review*, in an article by J. J. Tayler." This was probably the unsigned article on "The Harmony of the Intuitional and Logical Elements in the Ultimate Grounds of Religious Belief" in the *Prospective Review*, 1851, pp. 472 ff.

30. R. Williams, "Bunsen's Biblical Researches" in *Essays and Reviews*, 5th ed., 1861, p. 51.

31. R. Williams, loc. cit.

32. R. Williams, op. cit., p. 78.

33. R. Williams, loc. cit.

34. From an address delivered at Manchester College, Oxford, 12 October 1863, and reported in *The Christian Reformer*, November 1863, p. 662.

35. E. Abbott and L. Campbell, *The Life and Letters of Benjamin Jowett*, II, 1897, pp. 87–8.

36. H. R. Haweis, *Winged Words*, 1885, p. 248.

37. J. Martineau, *The Rationale of Religious Enquiry*, 1st ed., 1836, p. 17.

38. J. Martineau, loc. cit.

39. J. Martineau, op. cit., pp. 131–2.

40. J. Martineau, op. cit., pp. 132–3.

41. J. Blanco White, *The Life of the Rev. J. B. White*, edited by J. H. Thom, III, 1845, p. 106.

42. J. Blanco White, op. cit., III, pp. 131–2.

43. See passage from letter to A. Macdonald reported in J. E. Carpenter, *James Martineau*, 1905, p. 232, and from letter to Dr. Channing in J. E. Carpenter, op. cit., pp. 187–8. Both letters are dated 1840.

44. J. Martineau, *The Rationale of Religious Enquiry*, 3rd ed., 1845, p. viii of preface.

45. J. Martineau, loc. cit.

46. J. Martineau, *The Seat of Authority in Religion*, 4th ed., 1898, p. 577.

47. J. Martineau, op. cit., p. 592.

48. J. Martineau, loc. cit.

49. J. J. Tayler, *A Retrospect of the Religious Life of England*, 1st ed., 1845, p. 560.

50. C. C. Hennell, *Inquiry concerning the Origin of Christianity*, 1st ed., 1838, p. 154.

51. C. C. Hennell, op. cit., p. 149.

52. C. C. Hennell, op. cit., p. vi of preface.

53. W. R. Greg, *The Creed of Christendom*, 1851, p. 191.

54. W. R. Greg, op. cit., p. 206.

55. E. Higginson, *The Spirit of the Bible*, II, 1853, p. 85.

56. E. Higginson, loc. cit.

57. E. Higginson, op. cit., p. 87.

58. E. Higginson, loc. cit.

59. H. McLachlan, *The Unitarian Movement in the Religious Life of England*, 1934, p. 221.

60. *The Unitarian Herald*, 23 October 1863, p. 348.

61. *The Inquirer*, 29 October 1864, p. 705. See also T. Sadler, "The Unitarians of London between Forty and Fifty Years Ago", in *The Christian Reformer*, III, 1887, p. 151.

62. Walter Lloyd, "The Miracles of the Old and New Testaments", in *Religion and Modern Thought*, 1893, p. 68.

63. Walter Lloyd, op. cit., p. 69.

64. Stopford A. Brooke, *Life and Letters of F. W. Robertson*, II, 1891, p. 140.

65. Baden Powell, "On the Study of the Evidences of Christianity" in *Essays and Reviews*, 5th ed., 1861, p. 140.

66. Baden Powell, op. cit., p. 110.

67. Baden Powell, op. cit., p. 141.

68. Baden Powell, loc. cit.

69. Baden Powell, op. cit., p. 143.

70. Baden Powell, op. cit., p. 128.

71. E. Abbott and L. Campbell, *Life and Letters of Benjamin Jowett*, II, 1897, p. 87. Charles Voysey, who to some extent had been a "protégé" of Jowett said, in a sermon dated January 1868 (*Sling and the Stone*, III, 1868, p. 133), "It is now absolutely impossible for us to affirm that the miracles narrated in the Gospels ever took place at all."

72. E. Abbott and L. Campbell, op. cit., p. 311.

73. E. Abbott and L. Campbell, op. cit., p. 310.

74. A. H. Craufurd, *Recollections of James Martineau*, 1903, p. 65.

75. Matthew Arnold, *Literature and Dogma*, 4th ed., 1874, p. 148. *Literature and Dogma* was first published in the preceding year.

76. Matthew Arnold, op. cit., 1883 ed., concluding words of the preface.

77. *The Inquirer*, 4 December 1886, p. 788, said: "We welcome this book. . . . The matter is most valuable; the tone so candid and free from ill-temper, most delightful." *The Christian Reformer*, January 1887, p. 43, spoke of it as "a valuable contribution to the living religious thought of the present age".

78. E. A. Abbott, *The Kernel and the Husk*, 1886, p. 2.

79. See page 59 of this book.

80. E. A. Abbott, op. cit., p. 153.

81. E. A. Abbott, op. cit., p. 224.

82. P. 61 of this book.

83. Quoted in H. P. Liddon, *Life of Edward Bouverie Pusey*, IV, 1897, p. 54.

84. Lant Carpenter, *An Examination of Bishop Magee's Charges against Unitarians and Unitarianism*, 1820, p. 42.

85. W. R. Greg, *The Creed of Christendom*, 1851, p. 283.

86. *Prospective Review*, X, 1854, p. 13. The article entitled "Theories of Christian Salvation", like all articles appearing in the *Prospective*, was unsigned. The *Prospective Review*, published between 1845–54, and edited by J. J. Tayler, C. Wicksteed, J. Martineau, and J. H. Thom—all Unitarian ministers—reached, as A Gordon remarked in *Heads of English Unitarian History*, 1895, pp. 47–8, "the high watermark of Unitarian journalism"; and the eschatology of the article certainly expresses a Unitarian point of view.

87. *Prospective Review*, X, 1854, p. 15.

88. James F. Clarke, *Manual of Unitarian Belief*, 1884, p. 62.

89. H. S. Solly, "Punishment for Sin: Is it Eternal?" in *Religion and Modern Thought*, 1893, p. 155.

90. H. Crosskey, *The Unitarians*, 1888, p. 21.

91. Cf. Goblet d'Alviella, *The Contemporary Evolution of Religious Thought*, 1885, p. 66. See also L. P. Jacks, *Life and Letters of Stopford Brooke*, 1917, p. 174.

92. F. D. Maurice, *Theological Essays*, 1957, p. 307.

93. F. D. Maurice, op. cit., p. 323.

94. F. Warre Cornish, *A History of the English Church in the Nineteenth Century*, II, 1910, p. 202.

95. H. B. Wilson, "Séances Historiques de Genere" in *Essays and Reviews*, 5th ed., 1861, p. 206.

96. H. B. Wilson, loc. cit.

97. R. E. Prothero and G. G. Bradley, *The Life and Correspondence of A. P. Stanley*, II, 1893, p. 44.

98. J. W. Colenso, *Commentary on the Epistle to the Romans*, 1861, p. 177.

99. J. W. Colenso, loc. cit.

100. J. W. Colenso, op. cit., p. 180.

101. J. W. Colenso, op. cit., p. 187.

102. This was St. Mark's, Whitechapel. (See D. Wright in *Dictionary of National Biography*, *1912–1921*, pp. 545 ff., and *The New Schaff-Herzog Encyclopedia of Religious Knowledge*, ed. S. M. Jackson, 1912, XII, p. 230.) Voysey himself in *An Episode in the History of Religious Liberty in the 19th Century*, 1871, pp. 20–1, does not specify the name of the Church; but the *Oxford Dictionary of the Christian Church*, 1957, p. 1431, is incorrect when it states that the church was St. Mary's, Victoria Docks. Voysey was curate for a short time at a church at Victoria Docks, but this, like the one at Whitechapel, was called St. Mark's, and reference to Crockford's *Clerical Directory* shows that there was no church called St. Mary's at Victoria Docks.

103. C. Voysey, *An Episode in the History of Religious Liberty in the 19th Century*, 1871, pp. 20–1.

104. E. Abbott and L. Campbell, *Life and Letters of Benjamin Jowett*, I, 1897, p. 402, footnote.

105. B. Jowett, *Sermons on Faith and Doctrine*, ed. by W. H. Fremantle, 1901, p. 169.

106. C. Voysey, op. cit., p. 14.

107. L. P. Jacks, *Life and Letters of Stopford Brooke*, 1917, pp. 61–2.

108. L. P. Jacks, *Life and Letters of Stopford Brooke*, 1917, p. 305.

109. H. Tennyson, *Life of Alfred Lord Tennyson*, II, 1897, p. 90.

110. L. E. Elliott-Binns, *Religion in the Victorian Era*, 1936, p. 280.

111. Faustus Socinus (1539–1604) in his *De Jesu Christo Servatore*, 1594, attacked the satisfaction-theory of the Atonement.

112. John Kenrick, *Unitarianism the Essence of Vital Christianity*, 1817, p. 31.

113. J. Wright, *Denials and Beliefs of Unitarians*, 1901, p. 35. Note that, in spite of the date of publication, the contents, as the preface indicates, were prepared "many years ago" while Wright was minister at Bury, Lancashire; and in G. E. Evans, *Vestiges of Protestant Dissent*, 1897, p. 37, the date of Wright's ministry at Bury is given as 1853–73.

114. S. Bache, *The True Conditions of Christian Salvation. An Examination of the Sacrificial Efficacy of the death of Christ*, 1854, p. 49.

115. J. Wright, op. cit., p. 37.

116. J. Wright, op. cit., pp. 37–8.

117. E. Higginson, *The Sacrifice of Christ Scripturally and Rationally Interpreted*, 2nd ed., 1848, p. 47.

118. David Maginnis, *Characteristics of Christian Unitarianism*, 1859, pp. 9–10.

119. J. Martineau, *Studies of Christianity*, 1858, p. 476.

120. *The Inquirer*, 20 February 1886, pp. 122–3.

121. F. W. Robertson, *Sermons*, 1st series, 1883 ed., p. 136.

122. F. W. Robertson, loc. cit.

123. F. Arnold, *Robertson of Brighton*, 1886, p. 325.

124. Stopford A. Brooke, *Life and Letters of Frederick W. Robertson*, I, 1891 ed., pp. 303–4.

125. J. J. Tayler, *Retrospect of the Religious Life of England*, 2nd ed., 1876, p. 320.

126. J. J. Tayler, loc. cit.

127. F. J. Powicke, "F. D. Maurice—A Personal Reminiscence" in *The Congregational Quarterly*, 1930, p. 180.

128. F. D. Maurice, *Theological Essays*, 1957, p. 108.

129. F. D. Maurice, *The Doctrine of Sacrifice*, 1879 ed., p. 157.

130. F. J. Powicke, loc. cit.

131. Benjamin Jowett, *The Epistles of St. Paul to the Thessalonians, Galatians, and Romans*, II, 2nd ed., 1859, p. 547.

132. Benjamin Jowett, loc. cit.

133. Benjamin Jowett, op. cit., p. 566.

134. Benjamin Jowett, op. cit., p. 568.

135. Benjamin Jowett, op. cit., p. 568.

136. Benjamin Jowett, op. cit., p. 568.

137. Benjamin Jowett, op. cit., p. 568.

138. Benjamin Jowett, op. cit., p. 594.

139. J. W. Colenso, *Commentary on the Epistle to the Romans*, 1861, p. 93.

140. J. W. Colenso, loc. cit.

141. H. R. Haweis, *Winged Words*, 1885, p. 235. On p. 229 of the same work Haweis says: "The Substitution theory is absolutely false."

142. A. M. Ramsey, *F. D. Maurice and the Conflicts of Modern Theology*, 1951, p. 59.

143. W. H. Fremantle, *Natural Christianity*, 1911, p. 82. In spite of the date of publication, the book, as p. 10 of the Preface indicates, represents a much earlier point of view—in fact that of Fremantle over the preceding fifty years.

144. Hector Macpherson, *A Century of Intellectual Development*, 1907, p. 275.

145. Hector Macpherson, op. cit., p. 276. See also p. 305 of *An Examination of Canon Liddon's Bampton Lectures on the Divinity of our Lord and Saviour Jesus Christ, by a clergyman of the Church of England*, 1871.

146. Disbelief in miracles was an important factor in Stopford Brooke's abandonment of belief in the Incarnation and his final secession from the Church of England. See Stopford A. Brooke, *God and Christ*, 1894, pp. 328 and 340.

147. Stopford A. Brooke, *Life and Letters of Frederick W. Robertson*, II, new ed., 1891, pp. 161–2. Note also the following passage from a letter signed by "A Member of the Church of England" in *The Spectator*, 14 December 1867: "The doubt as to miracles, the doubt of Christ's Divinity, the doubt of the Resurrection, the doubt of the Inspiration (in any really weighty sense) of the Scriptures; all these doubts have spread wide and deep into the minds of thousands of earnest and noble-minded men, to whom a religion founded on the Creeds is no longer possible." And of Sydney Smith (1771–1845), who represents an earlier period, H. Pearson, in *Smith of Smiths*, 1934, p. 226, remarks, "Jesus Christ was for him a perfect type of man not a god, whose teachings were the acme of common sense and common humanity."

148. Stopford A. Brooke, op. cit., p. 162.

149. Stopford A. Brooke, loc. cit.

150. Stopford A. Brooke, op. cit., p. 161.

151. R. E. Prothero and G. G. Bradley, *Life and Letters of A. P. Stanley*, II, 1893, p. 163.

152. B. Jowett, *Epistles of St. Paul to the Thessalonians, Galatians, and Romans*, II, 2nd ed., 1859, p. 594.

153. B. Jowett, *Sermons on Faith and Doctrine*, ed. W. H. Fremantle, 1901, p. 203.

154. H. R. Haweis, *Winged Words*, 1885, p. 199.

155. J. W. Colenso, *Natal Sermons*, II, 1868, p. 150.

156. Possibly Charles Voysey. The Bodleian Library Catalogue entry bears a suggestion of his authorship. Another possibility is W. G. Clarke of Trinity College, Cambridge, who showed a similar viewpoint to the book with regard to the inconsistency of Protestants demanding adherence to articles of belief while allowing the right of private judgment.

157. *An Examination of Canon Liddon's Bampton Lectures on the Divinity of our Lord and Saviour Jesus Christ, by a clergyman of the Church of England*, 1871, p. 3. It is interesting to note that the writer was familiar with some Unitarian writings. See pp. 17–18.

158. *An Examination of Canon Liddon's Bampton Lectures on the Divinity of our Lord and Saviour Jesus Christ, by a clergyman of the Church of England*, 1871, p. 330.

159. The passage quoted is actually from the "Articles of Charge" brought against Voysey in his trial which began on 12 November 1870. (See R. T. Davidson and William Benham, *Life of Archibald Campbell Tait*, II, 1891, pp. 88–9.) The charge was not denied by Voysey, and that it accurately represents the doctrine of *The Sling and the Stone* may be seen from the following extracts: "I affirm that whatever Jesus was in his Divine and human natures, *that* he said we are also" (IV, 1869, p. 205); "There is no difference whatever in our relation to God between him (Jesus) and us" (IV, 1869, p. 206). Both extracts despite the date of publication in *The Sling and the Stone* are from a sermon preached on Christmas day, 1867, nearly three years before he was relieved of his position in the Anglican Church.

160. F. W. Cornish, *The English Church in the 19th Century*, II, 1910, pp. 241–2.

161. L. P. Jacks, *Life and Letters of Stopford Brooke*, 1917, p. 262. *The Inquirer*, 5 June 1869, in a report on the sermon preached by the Rev. C. Kegan Paul at the Free Christian Union Anniversary Service, represents the Broad Churchman as saying of himself and other Broad Churchmen, "It was sometimes asked how it was that they could consistently hold their positions in the Church, instead of going out boldly into the pure Theism which Christ taught. It was because they believed that Christ was a symbolical name for collective humanity, which they understood to be God."

162. Unitarians made much of the "leadership of Jesus". Thus *The Inquirer*, 1886, p. 264, stated of Unitarians: "They venerate Jesus as their spiritual leader, much as Mahometans (sic) venerate Mahomet and Jews venerate Moses"; and W. G. Tarrant in *Our Faith*, 1899, remarked, p. 56: "Of all the great teachers of mankind none has had such a powerful, such a good influence as Jesus of Nazareth."

163. W. H. Fremantle, "Is a Unitarian Entitled to Christian Fellowship?", *The Christian Reformer*, II, 1886, pp. 203–4.

164. W. H. Fremantle, op. cit., p. 204.

CHAPTER 4

1. Following his dismissal from the Church of England Voysey founded an independent congregation on 1 October 1871, and at the suggestion of Voysey the congregation assumed the title "Theistic Church" in 1880. A statement of the Theistic Church's aims may be seen on pp. 106–7 of G. d'Alviella, *The Contemporary Evolution of Religious Thought*, 1885. Its theology was essentially Unitarian.

2. G. d'Alviella, *The Contemporary Evolution of Religious Thought*, 1885, p. 105.

3. C. Voysey, *Revised Prayer Book*. The book went through several editions (1st, 1871; 2nd, 1875; 3rd, 1892) and is a modified form of the *Book of Common Prayer*.

4. R. E. Prothero and G. G. Bradley, *Life and Letters of A. P. Stanley*, II, 1893, pp. 16 and 231–5; A. P. Stanley, *The Life and Correspondence of Thomas Arnold*, II, 8th ed., 1858, p. 107.

5. *The Inquirer*, 7 July 1860, p. 565.

6. A. H. Craufurd, *Recollections of James Martineau*, 1903, p. 107.

7. A. H. Craufurd, op. cit., p. 108.

8. *Common Prayer for Christian Worship* was published in 1862 after Dr. Thomas Sadler had been commissioned to "revise the Services in use in the Church of England, and to make additions from other sources". See J. Drummond and C. B. Upton, *Life and Letters of James Martineau*, II, 1902, p. 380.

9. J. Drummond and C. B. Upton, op. cit., I, p. 386.

10. J. Drummond and C. B. Upton, loc. cit.

11. See Hymns 191–264 in J. Martineau, *Hymns for the Christian Church and Home*, 1840. The following hymns use the term "Redeemer": 193, 228, 229, 255, while the following use the word "Saviour": 196, 199, 201, 203, 208, 215, 216, 217, 220, 223, 224, 225, 231, 234, 255. The following hymns also use the term "Son of God": 217, 220, 221, 222.

12. See J. Martineau, *Hymns of Praise and Prayer*, 1874, hymns 126, 127, 131, 140.

13. J. Drummond and C. B. Upton, op. cit., p. 387.

14. J. Drummond and C. B. Upton, op. cit., p. 388.

15. From the canticle following the second lesson in the 10th service in *Common Prayer for Christian Worship*. The page is not numbered.

16. For example, H. L. Short.

17. See, for example, the frontispieces of J. Drummond and C. B. Upton, *Life and Letters of James Martineau*, I, II, 1902, and J. E. Carpenter, *James Martineau*, 1905.

18. J. Martineau, *Hymns of Praise and Prayer*, 1874, preface, p. xv.

19. W. D. Maxwell in *The Book of Common Prayer and the Worship of the Non-Anglican Churches*, 1950, p. 33, remarks: "The liturgical tradition in dissent was until recently almost wholly confined to the Unitarians." In 1882 John Hunter published his *Devotional Services for Public Worship*, which pioneered the way for some acceptance of liturgical forms of worship among Congregationalists. However, cf. Horton Davies, who in *Worship and Theology*, IV, 1962, p. 122 remarks that this "did not break the ice of Nonconformity's congealed adherence to extemporary prayers".

20. As W. B. Selbie remarks in *Nonconformity* (no date), p. 122: "It was the passing of this Act that made Nonconformity in this country."

21. W. D. Maxwell, *The Book of Common Prayer and the Worship of the Non-Anglican Churches*, 1950, p. 18: "Before 1753, Dissenters made no attempt that can definitely be traced to use anything but free prayer."

22. In reference to the Dissenting liturgical movement which followed the production of *A Specimen of a Liturgy*, 1753, W. D. Maxwell, in op. cit., pp. 19–20, remarks: "With only two exceptions, up to the third quarter of

the nineteenth century all of these dissenters' liturgies are Arian or Unitarian." The following is a list of all the liturgies mentioned by A. E. Peaston in *The Prayer Book Reform Movement in the XVIII Century*, 1940. All fall within the period 1753–1800 and all are unorthodox. (In some cases excessively lengthy titles have been abbreviated. Because in some cases the editor or editors are not known the place of publication is indicated throughout.)

1. *A Specimen of a Liturgy designed for use of a Private Congregation*, London, 1753;

2. P. Cardale, *A New Office of Devotion adapted to the Present Times*, London, 1758;

3. *The Christian Common Prayer Book or Universal Liturgy*, London, 1761;

4. J. Seddon, P. Holland, R. Godwin, *A Form of Prayer for a Congregation of Protestant Dissenters in Liverpool*, Liverpool, 1763;

5. T. Lindsey, *The Book of Common Prayer Reformed according to the plan of the late Dr. Samuel Clarke*, London, 1774, 1785, 1793;

6. D. Williams, *A Liturgy on the Universal Principles of Religion and Morality*, London, 1776;

7. *Forms of Prayer—collected, and a Liturgy selected from Book of Common Prayer*, Salisbury, 1776;

8. J. Priestley, *Forms of Prayer for the Use of Unitarian Societies*, Birmingham, 1783;

9. *Forms of Prayer for the use of a congregation of Dissenters in Manchester*, Birmingham, 1789;

10. Temple and Holmes, *The Book of Common Prayer Reformed upon Unitarian Principles*, Newcastle-on-Tyne, 1790;

11. *Forms of Prayer for Public Worship*, London, 1791;

12. S. Morgan, *A Common Prayer Book—according to Liturgy of the Church of England*, Exeter, 1791;

13. T. Porter, J. Kentish, *A Liturgy compiled from Book of Common Prayer reformed according to Dr. S. Clarke*, Plymouth, 1791;

14. J. Bretland, *A Liturgy for the use of the Mint Meeting in Exeter*, Exeter, 1792;

15. J. Disney, *Book of Common Prayer reformed for Unitarian Congregations*, London, 1792, 1802;

16. *Forms of Prayer used at Highbury Grove Chapel*, London, 1793;

17. B. Carpenter, *A Liturgy containing Forms of Devotion for each Sunday*, Stourbridge, 1793;

18. *Forms of Prayer for the use of a Congregation of Protestant Dissenters in Bradford*, Trowbridge, 1793;

19. *Devotional Offices collected from various sources in use among Dissenters*, Salisbury, 1794, 1810;

20. John Simpson, *A Form of Public Prayer for the Lord's Day*, Bath, 1794;

21. *Devotional Offices collected from various sources in use among Dissenters*, Shrewsbury, 1795, 1814;

22. *Devotional Offices for Protestant Dissenters at Mansfield*, Manchester, 1797.

To Mr. Peaston's list J. Harrison, *Specimens of the Manner in which Public*

Notes

Worship is conducted in Dissenting Congregations, Preston, 1793, should be added.

23. See the references to J. Hunter in note 19. Among the Methodists there was some use of liturgy, particularly, of course, in the celebration of the Lord's Supper, which John Wesley directed should be administered "according to the form of the Established Church". (See H. Bettenson, *Documents of the Christian Church*, 1956, p. 359.) But, on the whole, free prayer was much more characteristic of Methodism and in line with its charismatic tendency.

A very elaborate liturgy was used by the Catholic Apostolic Church, but the latter can only dubiously be placed within the ranks of Nonconformity, and is perhaps best confined to an ecclesiastical "no man's land" of its own.

24. A. E. Peaston, "Nineteenth Century Liturgies" in *Transactions of the Unitarian Historical Society*, VII, 1939–42, No. 3, p. 215.

25. The following is a list of the 56 liturgies produced by Unitarians between, and including, the dates 1801–1900. The list may not be complete, but it is nearly so.

1. W. Wood, *Forms of Prayer for Protestant Dissenting Congregations at Mill Hill Chapel*, Leeds, 1801;

2. J. T. Rutt, *Forms of Unitarian Worship for small Society of Protestant Dissent at Witham*, Sudbury, 1802, 1817;

3. T. Browne, *Eight forms of Prayer in Public Social Worship*, Bath, 1803;

4. T. Belsham, *The Book of Common Prayer Reformed*, London, 1805, 1813, 1820, 1822, 1823, 1824, 1835, 1836;

5. *Devotional Offices collected from various sources in use among Dissenters*, London, 1810;

6. W. Blake, Junr., *Devotional Services for the Public Worship of the One True God*, Sherbourne, 1812;

7. J. P. Estlin, *The General Prayer Book*, Bristol, 1814, 1817;

8. J. T. Rutt, *Liturgies for Unitarian Worship*, London, 1817;

9. *Forms of Prayer for the use of Congregation of Dissenters in Manchester*, London, 1817, 1839;

10. *Devotional Offices collected from various sources*, Poole, 1818;

11. *The Book of Common Prayer, corrected and arranged for Public Worship—at New Road Chapel, Brighton*, London, 1820;

12. *A Help to Scripture Worship altered according to Dr. S. Clarke*, Exeter, 1821;

13. W. Turner, *Offices of Public Worship for Unitarian Christians*, Newcastle, 1824;

14. R. Wallace, *Forms of Prayer for Unitarian Congregations*, Chesterfield, 1826;

15. *Devotional Offices from the Book of Common Prayer for Old Meeting House, Birmingham*, Birmingham, 1829, 1832, 1870;

16. T. Madge, *Book of Common Prayer revised for Public Worship*, London, 1836, 1839;

17. J. J. Tayler, *Forms of Prayer for Public Worship*, London, 1839, 1850;

18. *Book of Common Prayer reformed for Churches whose Worship is to the Father*, Manchester, 1841;

19. *Forms of Prayer for the use of English Presbyterian Congregations*, Ashton-under-Lyme, 1841, 1847;

20. W. J. Odgers, *Forms of Prayer for Public Worship*, London, 1844;

21. *Forms of Prayer for Christian Worship as used at Old Meeting, Great Yarmouth*, Yarmouth, 1844;

22. E. Tagart, *Book of Common Prayer revised for Public Worship*, London, 1846, 1848, 1849, 1865;

23. H. H. Piper, *Book of Common Prayer adapted for Other Protestant Churches*, London, 1852;

24. *Forms of Prayer for Unitarian Christians*, Bury, 1854;

25. *The Prayer Book of the Free Christian Church, Kentish Town*, London, 1855;

26. *Morning and Evening for Plymouth*, Plymouth, 1856;

27. *Forms of Prayer at Hackney*, Hackney, 1858, 1874;

28. G. Barmby, *Special Services for Churches of Christ*, Wakefield, 1859;

29. J. W. Lake, *Forms of Prayer for the Unitarian Chapel, Boston*, London, 1860;

30. J. R. Beard, *The Christian Year; A Service Book consisting of Passages of Scripture*, London, 1861;

31. R. Ainslie, *The Church Book for Christ Church, Brighton*, London, 1861, 1867;

32. T. Sadler and J. Martineau, *Common Prayer for Christian Worship*, London, 1862, 1873, 1886, 1895, 1900, 1910;

33. T. L. Marshall, *Book of Common Prayer revised for Public Worship*, London, 1867;

34. *Common Prayer adapted for all Christian Churches*, London, 1867;

35. *Book of Common Prayer revised* (Todmorden Liturgy), 1868;

36. G. Dawson, *The Book of Prayer and Praise in 14 Services*, Birmingham, 1970;

37. P. Dean, *Prayers and Ministries in 6 Services*, Walsall, 1878;

38. R. C. Jones, *30 Orders of Worship*, –, 1878, 5th ed., 1907;

39. T. Sadler, J. Martineau, P. H. Wicksteed, *Ten Services of Public Prayer*, London, 1879, 1884, 1887, 1907, 1916;

40. *Common Prayer for Newington Green*, London, 1884;

41. P. Dean, *Prayers and Ministries in 11 Services*, Walsall, 1885;

42. J. Wood, *A Book of Prayer in Ten Orders of Public Worship*, Birmingham, 1885, 1897, 5th ed., 1904;

43. S. Farrington, *Services of Experience and Hope*, Manchester, 1888;

44. Stopford Brooke, *The Form of Morning and Evening Prayer*, London, 1891;

45. J. Page Hopps, *A New Book of Common Prayer*, London, 1892;

46. F. E. Millson, *Our Book of Common Prayer*, Halifax, 1892;

47. V. Herford, E. S. Anthony, E. D. P. Evans, G. E. Evans, J. K. Pike, T. P. Spedding, *Morning Prayer; Evening Prayer; Text and Compline*, compiled at Kidderminster, 1893;

48. H. W. Pervis, *Forms of Prayer*, Hull, 1894;

49. E. P. Barrow, *Services of Prayer and Praise*, Manchester, 1894, 1902;

50. J. Wright, *Forms of Prayer for Bank Street, Bury*, Bury, 1896;

Notes

51. E. Fripp, *Common Prayer*, Mansfield, 1896?;

52. W. H. Drummond, T. Birchall, J. S. Hill, T. Whittle, W. H. Woodcock, F. W. Monks, *Four Orders of Warrington*, Warrington, 1896;

53. L. P. Jacks, *Six Orders of United Worship*, London, 1898;

54. R. Holt, S. Jones, *The Order for Morning and Evening Prayer*, Liverpool, 1899;

55. J. H. Green, *Five Orders of Prayer* (Lydgate Liturgy), Holinfirth, 1899;

56. W. C. Bowie, *Seven Services for Public Worship*, London?, 1900.

The majority of the above-mentioned liturgies that fall in the period 1801–54 will be found listed in the Chart at the back of A. E. Peaston's *Prayer Book Reform Movement*, 1940. A revised list, covering the same period, may be found in W. D. Maxwell, *The Book of Common Prayer and the Worship of the Non-Anglican Churches*, 1950, pp. 33–4, note 27. The present list covering the same period differs only slightly from both. For the complete list of the whole period (1801–1900) the present writer is deeply indebted to the very kind assistance of the Rev. A. E. Peaston.

26. The six liturgies that are not affected by the *Book of Common Prayer* are numbers 3, 30, 36, 37, 45, 53 in the list in the preceding note, namely, note 25.

27. The following liturgies, fifteen in all, went into two or more editions: 2, 4, 7, 9, 15, 16, 17, 19, 22, 27, 31, 32, 38, 39, 42. The numbers refer to the enumeration in note 25.

28. The three eighteenth-century liturgies, of which nineteenth-century editions were produced, were numbers 15, 19, and 21 in the list in note 22.

29. *Common Prayer for Christian Worship* was employed as the basis of a number of other liturgies including *Ten Services of Public Prayer* (1879), which was also widely used. See A. E. Peaston, "Nineteenth Century Liturgies" in *Transactions of the Unitarian Historical Society*, VII, 1939–42, pp. 219–20.

30. *Devotional Offices for Protestant Dissenters at Mansfield*, 1797, preface, p. iv.

31. The whole matter is discussed at length in Kenneth Clark, *The Gothic Revival*, first published in 1928. Shorter accounts may be found in A. L. Drummond, *The Church Architecture of Protestantism*, 1934, pp. 62 ff. and M. S. Briggs, *Architecture*, 1947, pp. 169 ff.

32. For Gothic buildings bricks could be used, which were much less expensive than the stone required for classical porticoes. See A. L. Drummond, op. cit., pp. 40–1.

33. The term "ecclesiology" came into use around 1840, and was used with regard to the idea that Church architecture should symbolize theological principles. Thus, for example, a triple window would stand for the Trinity. The term is particularly associated with the Cambridge Camden Society, which in 1841 brought out a monthly magazine entitled *The Ecclesiologist*. For further details, see Kenneth Clark, *The Gothic Revival*, 1962, pp. 150 ff.

34. Of the 214 churches built by the Church of England between 1818 and 1833 as a result of the Church Building Act of 1818, 174 were Gothic in style. See A. L. Drummond, op. cit., p. 65.

35. See H. L. Short, "Changing Styles in Nonconformist Architecture"

Notes

in *The Listener*, 17 March 1955, p. 473, who refers to the Unitarians as having "led the way" in the use of Nonconformist Gothic. So also Horton Davies, who is indebted to Short, speaks, in *Worship and Theology in England*, IV, 1962, p. 62, of the Unitarians as being "pioneers in the use of Gothic among the Nonconformists". Further research, involving inquiry to the headquarters of the Baptist Union, the Methodist Department for Chapel Affairs, the Congregational Memorial Hall, and correspondence with M. S. Briggs, author of *Puritan Architecture* and numerous other architectural works, and G. W. Dolbey, the Methodist architectural expert, have done nothing to affect Short's statement materially.

In the text of this book, however, such terms as "leaders" and "pioneers" have been carefully avoided in case they should be misinterpreted to mean that *no* Nonconformist Gothic can be found earlier than that first built by the Unitarians. This is not the case, and G. W. Dolbey informs the present writer, in private correspondence, that a Methodist church in Gothic style was built at Newbury in 1837. But such a case is only an isolated example, and the Unitarian examples are more concentrated and deliberate. Methodist Gothic did not really get under way until F. J. Jobson had published his *Chapel and School Architecture* (1850) in which he advocated the employment of this style.

All the major Nonconformist denominations made use of Gothic in the second half of the century, though, of course, Gothic did not come into universal use. Thus Briggs remarks, in *Puritan Architecture*, 1946, p. 38, that Gothic "seems first to have infected Nonconformity early in Queen Victoria's reign, but for another thirty or forty years many of the Dissenting chapels continued to be built in some variant of Roman or Greek architecture". Briggs mentions, on p. 40, op. cit., that the first very large Congregationalist Gothic Church to be built in London was Christ Church, Westminster Bridge, 1872. But the Unitarians had already built their, admittedly not so large, though more Gothic, Hampstead Church, London, ten years earlier in 1862. But, as previously indicated, in the second half of the century, Unitarians were not alone in desiring to make their churches, as Briggs puts it, p. 39, " 'look like churches' of the Anglican kind".

36. Briggs in op. cit., p. 39, states that Mill Hill, Leeds, "is said to have been the first (Nonconformist church) to be furnished with a proper chancel". But H. L. Short rightly states in "Changing Styles in Nonconformist Architecture" in *The Listener*, 17 March 1955, p. 473, that the first to have this was Gee Cross, Hyde. Thus in G. E. Evans, *Vestiges of Protestant Dissent*, 1897, pp. 109 and 127, the Hyde church is stated to have been opened on 5 July and the Leeds church on 27 December 1848. Mill Hill was one of the first Nonconformist churches to have stained glass windows.

37. A. L. Drummond, op. cit., p. 77.

38. The booklet, which is profusely illustrated, bears no date.

39. Flowery Field Church, in particular, has a rich, almost cathedral-like, atmosphere.

40. J. M. Neale and B. Webb, *Durandus*, 1843, Introduction, p. xxii.

41. A. P. Stanley, "The Religious Aspect of Gothic Architecture" in *Good Words*, 1878, p. 397.

42. A. P. Stanley, loc. cit.

43. T. Arnold, *Principles of Church Reform*, 2nd ed., 1833, p. 70.

CHAPTER 5

1. Note B. Jowett's remark in E. Abbott and L. Campbell, *Life and Letters of Benjamin Jowett*, I, 1897, p. 402, footnote, that it was "impossible for a clergyman holding liberal opinions to be too cautious in his mode of stating them". This would apply even more strongly with regard to acknowledgment of any Unitarian influence.

2. Note how R. Whately insisted that J. H. Thom should return the letters written by Whately to Blanco White, the Unitarian, which Thom had intended to include in his *Life of Blanco White*; and how, moreover, Whately did his best to prevent the publication of the book in order to save himself the embarrassment of public reference to the intimacy which existed between himself and the Unitarian. For an account of this see J. H. Thom, "Archbishop Whately and the Life of Blanco White" in the *Theological Review*, IV, 1867, pp. 82 ff.

3. Note, for example, how little reference is made to Blanco White in E. J. Whately's *Life and Correspondence of Richard Whately*, 1866; and also how small a space is given to the Unitarian phase of S. T. Coleridge's life in several biographies of him.

4. J. Gillman, *Life of S. T. Coleridge*, I, 1838, p. 65.

5. Coleridge became a Unitarian in 1793, but reverted to a Trinitarian position in 1807. See Cottle, *Reminiscences of Samuel Taylor Coleridge and Robert Southey*, 1847, p. 325, and also Coleridge's letter on pp. 314–25.

6. S. T. Coleridge, *Biographia Literaria*, ed. J. Shawcross, I, 1907, p. 114.

7. In a letter to Coleridge written in 1796 Lamb exclaims: "Coleridge! in reading your *Religious Musings* I felt a transient superiority over you. I *have* seen Priestley. I love to see his name repeated in your writings. I love and honour him almost profanely." *Letters of Charles Lamb*, I, 1888, p. 10.

8. S. T. Coleridge, *The Poetical Works of S. T. Coleridge*, ed. Rossetti (no date given), p. 55.

9. *Unpublished Letters from Samuel Taylor Coleridge to the Rev. John Prior Estlin*, ed. Henry A. Bright (no date given), p. 3. The letters range between the period 1796–1814 and constitute a valuable source of information regarding Coleridge's connection with Unitarianism.

10. For Coleridge's preaching at Birmingham see *Christian Reformer*, 1834, p. 838. For reference to Nottingham, see E. L. Griggs, *Unpublished Letters of Samuel Taylor Coleridge*, I, 1932, pp. 40–3.

11. J. Cottle, *Early Recollections*, I, 1837, p. 304.

12. Coleridge in a letter to Isaac Wood (a leading member of the Shrewsbury Unitarian Church) dated 19 January 1798, reproduced on pp. 838–40 of the *Christian Reformer*, 1834. The quoted passage occurs on p. 840.

13. *Unpublished Letters from Samuel Taylor Coleridge to the Rev. John Prior Estlin*, ed. Henry A. Bright (no date given), p. 99.

14. J. E. Carpenter, *James Martineau*, 1905, p. 127.

15. *Unpublished Letters from Samuel Taylor Coleridge to the Rev. John Prior Estlin*, ed. Henry A. Bright (no date given), p. 105.

16. J. Hunt, *Religious Thought in the Nineteenth Century*, 1896, p. 244. Cf. Coleridge, *Biographia Literaria*, ed. J. Shawcross, I, 1907, p. 137: "A more thorough revolution in my philosophic principles, and a deeper insight into my own heart, were yet wanting. Nevertheless, I cannot doubt, that the difference of my metaphysical notions from those of Unitarians in general contributed to my final re-conversion to the whole truth in Christ; even as according to his own confession the books of certain Platonic philosophers (libri quorundum Platonicorum) commenced the rescue of St. Augustine's faith from the same error aggravated by the far darker accompaniment of the Manichaean heresy."

17. V. F. Storr, *The Development of English Theology in the Nineteenth Century*, 1913, p. 333: "The closest disciple of Coleridge was Maurice . . . But his influence can be traced all down the century, and more immediately in those called Broad Churchmen, such as Arnold or Robertson." See also F. W. Farrar, who in his Bampton Lecture on the *History of Interpretation*, 1886, pp. 422 ff. declared: "If in later days the Church of England has made an immense advance (in theology) the progress is perhaps more due to Samuel Taylor Coleridge than to any ordained or professed theologian."

18. F. J. A. Hort in *Cambridge Essays*, 1856, p. 313, wrote of him: "An unquenchable thirst for liberty is the one unchanging spring of his whole life, always guided, but never checked by his equal reverence for law."

19. V. F. Storr, *The Development of English Theology in the Nineteenth Century*, 1913, p. 331: ". . . when Coleridge discusses the special doctrines of Christianity, the Atonement, the Trinity, and Original Sin, he treats of them mainly in their practical bearing." See also O. Pfleiderer, *The Development of Theology*, 1890, p. 310: "Coleridge illustrated his view of Christianity in its application to selected doctrines—original sin, redemption, baptism, inspiration. In doing this he everywhere seeks so far to rationalise the dogma as to surrender its scholastic husk while preserving its religious and moral kernel."

20. S. T. Coleridge, *Aids to Reflection*, ed. T. Fenby, 1877, pp. 234–5, 237. See O. Pfleiderer, op. cit., p. 310.

21. S. T. Coleridge, *Aids to Reflection*, ed. T. Fenby, 1877, p. 303, aphorism CXIX.

22. J. Gillman, *Life of S. T. Coleridge*, I. 1838, p. 165.

23. S. T. Coleridge, *Aids to Reflection*, ed. T. Fenby, 1877, p. 214. See J. Martineau, "Theology in Relation to Progressive Knowledge" in *Essays, Reviews and Addresses*, IV, 1891, p. 122: "If theologians could but look with a calm eye upon the past, they must see that, wherever the strife is over and the field is still, every advance of knowledge has been a gain to religion, won at the expense only of deforming fictions. As our petty schemes of the world break in pieces and fall away, diviner ones construct themselves and make us ashamed of our regrets. Who would now, in the interests of piety, wish to have back the childish little cosmos of the Hebrew legends, or the three storeys of the Pauline heaven? or dare to say, that, in superseding them, Copernicus and Newton blasphemed?"

24. See the reference, quoted earlier, to Priestley as "patriot, saint, and sage", which indicates Priestley's three-fold role as politician, minister, and scientist. In an undated letter to Estlin in *Unpublished Letters from Samuel Taylor Coleridge to the Rev. John Prior Estlin*, ed. Henry A. Bright, p. 69, Coleridge says, "I regard every experiment that Priestley made in Chemistry as giving *wings* to his more sublime theological works". It is interesting to note also that Estlin who had quite an influence on Coleridge in the early part of his career was, as Brandt calls him in *Life of Coleridge*, 1887, p. 113, "a lover of science".

25. J. Gillman, *Life of S. T. Coleridge*, I, 1838, p. 155.

26. *The Oxford Dictionary of the Christian Church*, ed. F. L. Cross, 1957, p. 309. Julia Wedgwood in *Nineteenth Century Teachers*, 1909, in an article entitled "Samuel Taylor Coleridge", which originally appeared in the *Contemporary Review*, April 1895, seems to wish ("we would venture to describe him as the father of the Broad Church") to be thought of as having originated the phrase. But it was known to H. Solly in 1893. See H. Solly, *These Eighty Years*, I, 1893, p. 387.

27. F. Maurice, *Life of Frederick Denison Maurice*, II, 4th ed., 1885, p. 15.

28. Mrs. George Boole, "Maurice and the National Church" in *Dublin University Magazine*, I, 1878, p. 720. Formerly Miss Everest, Mrs. George Boole, wife of Professor George Boole, Professor of Mathematics at Cork, whom she married in 1855, was keenly interested in Maurice's religious position and had many religious discussions with him.

29. Mrs. George Boole, loc. cit.

30. H. G. Wood, *Frederick Denison Maurice*, 1950, p. 27.

31. Delivered in 1846, and published in the following year.

32. F. J. Powicke, "F. D. Maurice—A Personal Reminiscence" in *Congregational Quarterly*, April 1930, p. 180.

33. *Memorable Unitarians*, 1906, p. 199. Rammohun Roy (1772–1833), the founder of the Hindu reforming sect, "Brahmo-Samaj", came to England—the first high-caste Hindu to do so—in 1830, and was much revered by Unitarians. See E. M. Wilbur, *A History of Unitarianism in Transylvania, England, and America*, 1952, pp. 348 ff.; *Memorable Unitarians*, 1906, pp. 199 ff, and A. C. Bouquet, *Hinduism*, 1948, pp. 122 ff.

Another Indian visitor who received friendly interest from Unitarians was Keshub Chunder Sen, who visited England in 1870. Martineau allowed him to preach from his pulpit. See J. E. Carpenter, *James Martineau*, 1905, p. 436, J. Drummond and C. B. Upton, *Life and Letters of James Martineau*, II, 1902, pp. 2 ff.

Unitarians, it should be added, have been conspicuous in such organizations as "The World Congress of Faiths", and for many years readings from non-Christian religious writings have been a permissible and fairly common feature of their religious services. Thus, writing as early as 1885 Count Goblet d'Aviella observed regarding this matter that "some of the ministers of the advanced type . . . no longer select their reading lessons exclusively from the Old and New Testaments, but also from what the Rev. Peter Dean calls the sacred literature of all ages and peoples". See Goblet d'Aviella, *Contemporary Evolution of Religious Thought*, 1885, p. 92.

34. H. G. Wood, *Frederick Denison Maurice*, 1950, p. 36.

35. See F. Maurice, *Theological Essays*, 3rd ed., 1871, p. 403: "The world is the Church without God; the Church is the world restored to its relation with God, taken back by him into the state for which he created it"; also *Sermons Preached in Lincoln's Inn Chapel*, V, 1891, p. 241, the preacher may say to all men: "Of your relation to this Church you cannot rid yourselves, any more than you can change the law under which your natural bodies . . . exist. It is one which you must confess along with us, because you are human beings as well as we are."

36. See F. Maurice, *Life of Frederick Denison Maurice*, II, 4th ed., 1885, p. 358: "Mankind stands not in Adam but in Christ". See F. Maurice, *Life of Frederick Denison Maurice*, I, 4th ed., 1885, p. 198. Also A. R. Vidler, *Theology of F. D. Maurice*, 1948, p. 79: ". . . Maurice did not accept that sharp differentiation between nature and grace, or between the natural and the supernatural, or between humanity and the redeemed humanity that seems to underlie much received theology." Also, p. 80: "He held that God is in living relation with all men, that no man is merely 'natural'."

37. A. R. Vidler, *Theology of F. D. Maurice*, 1948, pp. 13 ff.

38. H. G. Wood, *Frederick Denison Maurice*, 1950, p. 26. Michael Maurice, F. D. Maurice's father, attended Hoxton Academy from 1782 until it closed in 1785. He then removed to the new founded Hackney College in 1786, where he remained till 1787. See *Life of Frederick Denison Maurice*, I, 4th ed., 1885, p. 7. For further details of Hoxton see H. McLachlan, *English Education under the Test Acts*, 1931, pp. 117 ff.

39. R. E. Prothero and G. G. Bradley, *Life and Correspondence of Arthur Penrhyn Stanley*, II, 1893, p. 168. From a letter dated 10 March 1864.

40. T. Wright, *Life of Walter Pater*, I, 1907, p. 136. For Liddon's part in this, see T. Wright, op. cit., I, p. 207. Both Dean Stanley and Professor Jowett were supporters of Pater.

41. F. J. Powicke, "F. D. Maurice—A Personal Reminiscence" in *The Congregational Quarterly*, VIII, No. 2, April 1930, p. 175.

42. F. J. Powicke, op. cit., p. 176.

43. F. Maurice, *Life of Frederick Denison Maurice*, I, 4th ed., 1885, p. 13.

44. F. Maurice, op. cit., II, p. 412.

45. F. Maurice, op cit., II, p. 413.

46. G. V. Jacks on Stopford Brooke in *D.N.B.* (1912–21), p. 68.

47. C. P. S. Clarke, *Short History of the Christian Church*, 3rd ed. (3rd impression), 1956, p. 477.

48. L. P. Jacks, *Life and Letters of Stopford Brooke*, 1917, p. 42.

49. L. P. Jacks, loc. cit.

50. R. W. Emerson, *Works of Ralph Waldo Emerson*, published by George Routledge and Sons (no date), p. 575.

51. L. P. Jacks, *Life and Letters of Stopford Brooke*, 1917, p. 203.

52. Stopford A. Brooke, *Sermons Preached in St. James' Chapel (Second Series)*, 7th ed., 1891, p. 311.

53. L. P. Jacks, op. cit., pp. 77–8.

54. L. P. Jacks, op. cit., p. 115.

55. L. P. Jacks, op. cit., p. 119.

Notes

56. J. Martineau, "Tracts for Priests and People" in *Essays, Reviews and Addresses*, II, 1891, p. 443.

57. Stopford A. Brooke, *Sermons Preached in St. James' Chapel*, First Series, 13th ed., 1883, p. 110.

58. L. P. Jacks, op. cit., p. 324.

59. L. P. Jacks, op. cit., p. 435.

60. J. Drummond and C. B. Upton, *Life and Letters of James Martineau*, II, 1902, p. 48.

61. J. Drummond and C. B. Upton, *Life and Letters of James Martineau*, II, 1902, pp. 471–2.

62. So Brooke said to Princess Alice: " 'Ah, Madame', said I, 'if I am anything, I owe what I am to Robertson' "—L. P. Jacks, *Life and Letters of Stopford Brooke*, 1917, p. 169. See also L. P. Jacks, op. cit., p. 62.

63. *Endeavours after the Christian Life*—a collection of sermons by James Martineau. The First Series was published in 1843 and the Second in 1847. In 1866 the Fourth Edition was published incorporating both series.

64. J. Hoatson, "James Martineau and Frederick Robertson" in *Expositor*, 1903, p. 204.

65. *Expositor*, loc. cit.

66. Stopford Brooke, *Life of F. W. Robertson*, II, 1891, p. 197.

67. The following extracts will give some idea of the influence which may be discerned. Besides the general drift of each passage there are a number of verbal and conceptual similarities, some of which have been italicized. The quoted passages are from J. Martineau, *Endeavours*, 10th impression, 1900, and F. W. Robertson, *Sermons*, 1st Series, ed. 1883.

MARTINEAU	ROBERTSON
"To a *wise*[1] man there is no *surer mark*[2] of decline in the *spirit of a people*,[3] than the corruption of their language and *the loss of meaning*[4] from their highest and most sacred words. . . . Observe, for example, the lowered *meaning of the word*[5] Religion." P. 251.	"Words had *lost their meaning*[4] . . . This is the period in which every keen and *wise*[1] observer knows that the decay of *national*[3] religious feeling has begun. That decay in the *meaning of words*,[5] that lowering of the standard of the ideas for which they stand, is a *certain mark*[2] of this. . . . The Name of God shares this fate." P. 43.
"In answer to the earnest *cry*[1] of society, 'What shall we do to be saved from all our miseries and *sins?*'[2] there are countless fragmentary answers, in place of the deep full of harmony of response, *from the soul*[3] of Christian inspiration. 'Give us more *bread*',[4] says one." P. 263.	"What is the *cry*[1] that comes *from the most real part of his nature?*[3] Is it the cry for daily *bread?*[4] . . . Is it even this,—to be forgiven our *sins?*"[2] P. 45.

157

Both of the above pairs of extracts, it should be added, are from the same two sermons. But often Robertson drew ideas from more than one sermon. Thus the following passage in the same sermon shows the influence of another passage in Martineau.

MARTINEAU

"So are *words*[1] great *powers*[2] in this world; not only telling what things are, but making them what else they would not be: and they cannot encroach upon the sphere of silence, without . . . *banishing the presence of God*."[3] P. 493.

ROBERTSON

"In this, too, seems to lie a most important truth. *Names*[1] have a *power*,[2] a strange power of *hiding God*."[3] P. 48.

68. Stopford Brooke, op. cit., II, pp. 102–3.

69. J. Hoatson, "James Martineau and Frederick Robertson" in *The Expositor* (6th Series), VIII, 1903, pp. 217–8.

70. H. Solly, *These Eighty Years*, II, 1893, p. 34.

71. F. P. Cobbe, *Darwinism in Morals and other Essays*, 1872, pp. 105–6. From the Essay "An English Broad Churchman" which originally appeared in the *Theological Review*, January, 1866.

72. F. P. Cobbe, op. cit., p. 106.

73. Stopford Brooke, *Life of F. W. Robertson*, I, New ed., 1891, p. 106.

74. Stopford Brooke, *Life of F. W. Robertson*, I, New ed., 1891, p. 102.

75. *Expositor*, 1903, p. 205.

76. Stopford A. Brooke, *Life of F. W. Robertson*, I, 1891, pp. 106, 115.

77. *Expositor*, 1903, p. 205.

78. H. Crabb Robinson, *Diary, Reminiscences, and Correspondence of Henry Crabb Robinson*, selected and edited by Thomas Sadler, III, 1869, p. 281.

79. H. Crabb Robinson, op. cit., III, p. 230.

80. H. Crabb Robinson, op. cit., III, p. 315.

81. H. Crabb Robinson, op. cit., III, p. 409.

82. H. Crabb Robinson, op. cit., III, p. 375.

83. See note 29 in Chapter 3 of this book. This identity of view, of course, is not proof of borrowing, but it does suggest the possibility of receptivity to Tayler's ideas.

84. H. Crabb Robinson, op. cit., III, p. 432. (Letter dated 25 December 1854.)

85. Frederick Arnold, *Robertson of Brighton*, 1886, p. 155.

86. H. Crabb Robertson, op. cit., III, p. 432.

87. Stopford Brooke, *Life of F. W. Robertson*, II, 1891, p. 163.

88. F. Arnold, *Robertson of Brighton*, 1886, p. 302. See also H. Crabb Robinson, op. cit., III, p. 300.

89. Stopford A. Brooke, *Life and Letters of the Rev. F. W. Robertson*, II, New ed., 1891, p. 163.

90. Stopford A. Brooke, op. cit., I, p. 283.

91. Stopford A. Brooke, op. cit., II, pp. 162–3.

92. Stopford A. Brooke, *Life of F. W. Robertson*, I, 1891, p. 324.

93. J. W. Chadwick, *William Ellery Channing*, 1903, p. 437.

94. The notes on which Robertson's address at Hurstpeirpoint in 1851

was based appear on pp. 259 ff. of his *Lectures and Addresses on Literary and Social Topics*, 1858. See Stopford Brooke, *Life of F. W. Robertson*, II, 1891, p. 18.

95. Brooke Herford, "Channing and His Work", in *Religion and Modern Thought* (Collection of Essays—no editor, published 1893), p. 119.

96. J. W. Chadwick, *William Ellery Channing*, 1903, p. 194.

97. Sydney Smith stood for "a free altar, an open road to heaven" (Hesketh Pearson, *Smith of Smiths*, 1934, p. 137), and he thought of the Church of England as "a Branch of the Civil Service" (op. cit., p. 227). "Christianity was for him a moral code, not a dogma" (op. cit., p. 226).

98. J. W. Chadwick, *William Ellery Channing*, 1903, p. 195.

99. Hesketh Pearson, *Smith of Smiths*, 1934, p. 243.

100. *The Centenary Commemoration of the Birth of Dr. William Ellery Channing*, 1880 (published by the British and Foreign Unitarian Association), p. 21.

101. Ibid., p. 245.

102. *The Methodist*, 16 April 1880. Quoted in *The Centenary Commemoration of the Birth of Dr. William Ellery Channing*, 1880, p. 245.

103. Brooke Herford, "Channing and his Work" in *Religion and Modern Thought* (Collection of Essays—no editor—1893), p. 124.

104. *The Centenary Commemoration of the Birth of Dr. William Ellery Channing*, 1880, p. 76.

105. *The Inquirer*, 25 March 1871, p. 181.

106. *The Expositor*, VIII, 1903, p. 218.

107. John Hunt, *Religious Thought in England in the Nineteenth Century*, 1896, p. 234.

108. Quoted, without indicating the source, on pp. 39–40 of G. W. Cox, *Life of Bishop Colenso*, II, 1888. The passage is found on p. 42 of J. Martineau's *Endeavours* (Tenth Impression—1900).

109. G. W. Cox, *Life of Bishop Colenso*, II, 1888, p. 40.

110. For example, F. P. Cobbe, Mary Carpenter.

111. J. Drummond and C. B. Upton, *Life and Letters of James Martineau*, II, 1902, pp. 26 ff.

112. A. H. Craufurd, *Recollections of James Martineau*, 1903, p. 3.

113. This invitation produced much indignation in certain Church circles at the time. For an account see R. E. Prothero and G. G. Bradley, *Life of Dean Stanley*, II, 1893, pp. 216 ff.

It is interesting to note that Henry Solly, the Unitarian minister, once took Communion at F. D. Maurice's church, and, though, as Solly remarks (see H. Solly, *These Eighty Years*, II, 1893, pp. 271–2), Maurice's son later informed him that his father had taken this act to mean that he (Solly) had become a member of the Church of England, the following passages suggest Maurice would not have debarred Solly had he known that he was still a Unitarian. Thus Mrs. George Boole wrote of Maurice in "Maurice and the National Church" in *The Dublin University Magazine*, 1878, p. 590: "Once I put to him this question: Supposing the person to whom he most objected (I instanced M. Renan if residing in England) came and said, 'I do not understand your sermons, and I do not believe your creeds; but I believe common worship is a means of promoting charity among those who differ,

and I mean to present myself for Communion at your church next Sunday'
—I took care not to say, 'Would you *admit* him', I worded it carefully:—
'Would you not say that he had just exactly all the right there that you have
yourself?' After a pause, Mr. Maurice answered, 'Of course I should'."
She added later, on pp. 590–1, that Maurice had preached a sermon in
which "he expressed his wish that the laity would assert their right to Communion in spite of whatever the clergy might say"; and she continued:
"When he made that request . . . he at least knew it would be taken by
several people . . . not as implying a vague and mystical assertion about the
ideal possibility of a Universal Church in which everyone should see the
Resurrection from the right point of view; but as an answer to a question
about the actual and immediate right to Communion of a man who believed
the miracles to be conjuring tricks."

114. J. Drummond and C. B. Upton, op. cit., II, p. 93.

115. Letter of Martineau to W. Knight, and dated 10 August 1881. In
the Knight letters at Manchester College, Oxford.

116. J. Drummond and C. B. Upton, op. cit., II, p. 91.

117. J. E. Carpenter, *James Martineau*, 1905, p. 530.

118. A. H. Craufurd, *Recollections of James Martineau*, 1903, pp. 64,
230.

119. G. Faber, *Jowett—A Portrait with background*, 1957, p. 303.

120. F. P. Cobbe, *Life of Frances Power Cobbe*, I, 1894, p. 351.

121. F. P. Cobbe, op. cit., I, p. 356.

122. F. P. Cobbe, op. cit., I, p. 349.

123. F. P. Cobbe, op. cit., II, p. 158.

124. G. W. Cox, *Life of Bishop Colenso*, I, 1888, p. 246.

125. V. D. Davis, *A History of Manchester College*, 1932, p. 172.

126. V. D. Davis, op. cit., pp. 186–7.

127. A. H. Craufurd, *Recollections of James Martineau*, 1903, p. 166.

128. H. Solly, *These Eighty Years*, II, 1893, p. 93.

129. H. Solly, op. cit., p. 94.

130. H. Solly, op. cit., II, pp. 136, 151.

131. H. Solly, op. cit., II, p. 138.

132. H. Solly, op. cit., II, p. 151.

133. H. Solly, op. cit., II, p. 126.

134. H. Solly, op. cit., II, p. 270.

135. H. Solly, op. cit., II, p. 268.

136. H. Solly, op. cit., II, p. 191.

137. L. P. Jacks, *The Confession of an Octogenarian*, 1942, p. 99.

138. L. P. Jacks, op. cit., p. 84.

139. L. P. Jacks, op. cit., pp. 84–5, 227.

140. *Free Christian Union Papers*—24.133 (22). In Dr. Williams's Library,
London.

141. J. E. Carpenter, *Life and Work of Mary Carpenter*, 1881, p. 243.

142. Ibid., p. 196.

143. *The Inquirer*, 19 May 1860, p. 413.

144. See the references to Rev. J. Moden in *The Inquirer*, 25 September
1886, pp. 628–9, under the editorial, "A Broad-Church Seceder".

145. H. Solly, *These Eighty Years*, II, 1893, p. 206.

146. R. A. Armstrong, *H. W. Crosskey, His Life and Work*, 1895, p. 159.

147. J. H. Thom, *Life of the Rev. Joseph Blanco White, written by himself*, I, 1845, p. 349.

148. J. H. Thom, op. cit., I, p. 346.

149. J. H. Thom, op. cit., I, p. 349.

150. J. H. Thom, op. cit., I, p. 356.

151. J. Blanco White, *Observations on Heresy and Orthodoxy*, 1835, preface vi.

152. T. Mozley, *Reminiscences Chiefly of Oriel College and the Oxford Movement*, II, 1882, p. 359. Also, G. Faber, *Oxford Apostles*, ed. 1954, pp. 175–6.

153. A. Hore in *The Church in England from William III to Victoria*, II, 1886, p. 255, speaks of Blanco White as having "materially affected the theology of Oriel". J. W. C. Wand similarly remarks in *A History of the Modern Church*, 1955, p. 208: "Blanco White . . . contributed both a knowledge of Roman Catholicism from within, and also an essentially sceptical outlook." Note also R. W. Church's reference in *The Oxford Movement*, 1891, p. 15, to Blanco White's having "sowed the seeds of doubt around him" at Oriel. See also pp. 129–30 in op. cit.

154. H. P. Liddon, *Life of E. B. Pusey*, I, 1893, p. 360.

155. H. P. Liddon, loc. cit.

156. J. H. Newman, *Apologia pro Vita sua*, 1864, ed., p. 65.

157. R. D. Hampden, *The Scholastic Philosophy considered in its relation to Christian Theology*, 2nd ed., 1837, p. 378.

158. R. D. Hampden, op. cit., p. 379.

159. R. D. Hampden, *Observations on Religious Dissent*, 1834, p. 21.

160. R. D. Hampden, loc. cit.

161. Thus, for example, G. Faber, who minimizes Blanco White's influence, admits of Hampden's lectures that "the special line of thought which he took for his own was perhaps originally suggested to him by Blanco White". See G. Faber, *Oxford Apostles*, 1954, p. 337. Cf. S. C. Carpenter, *Church and People (1789–1889)*, 1933, p. 148: "The Lectures had been largely prompted by Blanco White. . . ."

162. J. H. Thom, *Life of the Rev. Joseph Blanco White*, III, 1845, p. 362.

163. J. Blanco White, *Observations on Heresy and Orthodoxy*, 1835, preface, p. v.

164. J. Blanco White, op. cit., p. 9.

165. T. Mozley, *Reminiscences Chiefly of Oriel College and the Oxford Movement*, I, 1882, p. 373.

166. T. Mozley, op. cit., II, p. 354.

167. T. Mozley, op. cit., II, p. 353.

168. W. Tuckwell, *Pre-Tractarian Oxford*, 1909, p. 136.

169. T. Mozley, op. cit., II, p. 360.

170. T. Mozley, op. cit., II, p. 352.

171. H. P. Liddon, *Life of Edward Bouverie Pusey*, I, 1893, p. 360.

CHAPTER 6

1. Thomas Arnold, *Principles of Church Reform*, 4th ed., 1833, pp. 28–9

2. Thus Arnold says, on p. 79 of op. cit., "I am anxious to secure a tr

national church, which, uniting within itself all Christians who deserved the name, except perhaps the mere handful of the Quakers andRomanCatholics, would leave without its pale nothing but voluntary or involuntary godlessness."

3. Thomas Arnold, op. cit., pp. 66–71.

4. For example: S. C. Carpenter, *Church and People, 1789–1889*, 1937, p. 63; and F. W. Cornish, *The English Church in the Nineteenth Century*, I, 1910, p. 189.

5. T. Arnold, op. cit., p. 36.

6. T. Arnold, op. cit., p. 37.

7. T. Arnold, op. cit., p. 96. In a letter dated 22 June 1838, Arnold stated that "the most decided Socinian" might subscribe to the Thirty-Nine Articles "as consistently" as Keble or Newman. See A. P. Stanley, *The Life and Correspondence of Thomas Arnold*, II, 8th ed., 1858, p. 108. Cf. the passage from J. Hey, note 61, Chapter 1, of this book.

8. R. E. Prothero and G. G. Bradley, *Life and Correspondence of A. P. Stanley*, I, 1893, p. 116.

9. R. E. Prothero and G. G. Bradley, op. cit., II, pp. 278 ff. See especially p. 280.

10. Stanley's long-standing dislike of the terms of clerical subscription found embodiment in his *A Letter to the Lord Bishop of London on the State of Subscription in the Church of England and in the University of Oxford*, which was published as a pamphlet in 1863 and was not without influence in bringing about the Clerical Subscription Act of 1865, which relaxed the terms of subscription.

Several years later, after the Act had been passed, Stanley expressed the view, on p. xx of the preface to his *Essays chiefly on Church and State*, 1870, that "there can be no question that the change from the present form of test to the entire removal of any form, would be less" than that from "the stringent and elaborate system which existed formerly to the test as now modified".

11. R. E. Prothero and G. G. Bradley, *Life and Correspondence of A. P. Stanley*, II, 1893, pp. 538 ff. See also R. E. Prothero in *Dictionary of National Biography*, LIV, 1898, p. 47.

12. A. P. Stanley, *Addresses and Sermons delivered during a visit to the United States and Canada in 1878*, 1883, pp. 8–9.

13. H. B. Wilson, "Seances Historiques de Geneve. The National Church", in *Essays and Reviews*, 5th ed., 1861, p. 195.

14. H. B. Wilson, op. cit., p. 194.

15. H. B. Wilson, op. cit., p. 180.

16. H. B. Wilson, op. cit., p. 173.

17. W. G. Clark, *True and False Protestantism*, 1871, pp. 28–9.

18. *The Inquirer*, 2 January 1886, p. 4, in an article entitled "The Church of the Future", by F. A. Paley.

19. H. Alford, *Essays and Addresses—chiefly on Church Subjects*, 1869, p. 100.

20. H. Alford, loc. cit.

21. G. H. Curteis, *Dissent and its Relation to the Church of England*, 1871, p. 330.

22. G. H. Curteis, op. cit., p. 318.

23. W. H. Fremantle, "Is a Unitarian entitled to Christian Fellowship?", in *The Christian Reformer*, II, 1886, p. 204.

24. The terms "unwilling Dissenter" and "unwilling Nonconformist" were often used by Unitarians in describing themselves, and, after referring to a letter in which Martineau spoke of himself in the latter terms, a leading article entitled "Unwilling Nonconformist" in *The Inquirer*, 6 February 1886, p. 88, stated: "Many Unitarians, no doubt, would describe themselves by the same terms."

25. See J. Martineau's letter to E. S. Anthony, dated 11 May 1888, in J. Drummond and C. B. Upton, *Life and Letters of J. Martineau*, II, 1902, p. 143.

26. T. Belsham, in a pamphlet consisting of three sermons entitled *Christianity Pleading for the Patronage of the Civil Power, but Protesting against the Aid of Penal Laws*, 1820, p. 15. "Whoever assents to these propositions", said Belsham, "is a Christian, whatever additional articles he may affirm or deny."

27. H. Crabb Robinson, *Diary*, II, 1869, p. 128.

28. The details are conveniently summarized in Wilbur, *A History of Unitarianism in Transylvania, England and America*, 1952, pp. 356 ff., and in Wilbur, *Our Unitarian Heritage*, 1925, pp. 376–7 and 380 ff.

29. See note 10 in Chapter 1 of this book.

30. J. Drummond and C. B. Upton, *Life and Letters of J. Martineau*, I, 1902, p. 371.

31. J. Martineau, *Essays, Reviews and Addresses*, II, 1891, pp. 382–2.

32. J. Drummond and C. B. Upton, *Life and Letters of J. Martineau*, II, 1902, p. 142.

33. J. Drummond and C. B. Upton, loc. cit. Martineau tried to popularize the term "English Presbyterian" in respect of congregations.

34. J. Martineau, *Essays, Reviews and Addresses*, II, 1891, p. 372.

35. J. Martineau, *Essays, Reviews and Addresses*, II, 1891, p. 379.

36. An account of the affairs of the Free Christian Union may be found in J. Drummond and C. B. Upton, op. cit., I, pp. 415–36. The papers of the Free Christian Union, which have been consulted in this study, are kept at Dr. Williams's Library, 14 Gordon Square, London, W.C.1.

37. As indicated in note 15 in Chapter 1 the term "catholic", as used by the English Presbyterians, meant comprehension and mutual toleration. The term was inherited from them by Martineau and Tayler, and used as a protest against the Unitarian "sectarianism" of Unitarian converts who brought over with them the denominationalistic spirit of their former orthodoxy. For Martineau and Tayler a "catholic" church was a "broad" church capable of comprehending different points of view.

The origin of this development of the meaning of the term appears to be William Perkins' *A Reformed Catholike*, 1597, which urged that there was a basic Christian orthodoxy which Calvinists possessed in a pure form and the Romanists in a perverted form. The idea of a simple basic orthodoxy was taken up by Baxter and used in the interests of comprehension and toleration.

38. J. Drummond and C. B. Upton, op. cit., I, p. 428.

39. It is interesting to note that in a letter dated 8 November 1867, and preserved among the Free Christian Union Papers (Reference 24.133 [35]) in Dr. Williams's Library, Kegan Paul expressed some doubt regarding the use of the term "Christian" in reference to the purpose of the Free Christian Union because he was "not sure that the religion of the future will honestly be able to call itself Christian".

40. J. J. Tayler, *A Catholic Church the Want of Our Time*, 1867, p. 12.

41. This passage, which comes from a letter to Julius Hare, dated 26 January 1835, and reproduced in A. P. Stanley's *Life and Correspondence of Thomas Arnold*, I, 8th ed., 1858, p. 331, is included under the reference number 24.133 (4) among the Free Christian Union Papers in Dr. Williams's Library, London, regarding draft schemes setting forth the purpose of the Free Christian Union, which latter, seeing that "uniformity in doctrinal opinion becomes ever more precarious, while moral and spiritual affinities grow and deepen", sought to relieve "the Christian life from reliance on theological articles". A fuller statement of the Free Christian Union's aims may be seen in J. Drummond and C. B. Upton, op. cit., I, 1902, p. 427. Other passages from Dr. Arnold are included among the same set of Free Christian Union papers.

42. J. Drummond and C. B. Upton, op. cit., I, pp. 435–6.

43. J. Drummond and C. B. Upton, op. cit., II, pp. 108 ff.

44. J. Drummond and C. B. Upton, op. cit., II, p. 110; "Ecclesiastical Notes" in *The Christian Reformer*, I, 1886, p. 189.

45. J. Drummond and C. B. Upton, op. cit., II, pp. 108–9. R. Bosworth Smith was a master at Harrow School.

46. J. Drummond and C. B. Upton, op. cit., II, p. 109.

47. Reprinted in J. Martineau, *Essays, Reviews and Addresses*, II, 1891. p. 539.

48. J. Drummond and C. B. Upton, op. cit., II, pp. 116 ff.

49. J. Martineau, *Essays, Reviews and Addresses*, II, 1891, p. 567.

50. J. Martineau, op. cit., II, p. 575.

51. J. Martineau, op. cit., II, p. 556.

52. J. Martineau, op. cit., II, pp. 567–8.

53. J. Martineau, op. cit., II, p. 575.

54. J. Martineau, op. cit., I, p. 50.

55. J. Martineau, op. cit., II, pp. 525 ff. The essay was originally published in *The Christian Reformer*, February 1886.

56. J. Martineau, op. cit., II, p. 538.

57. J. Martineau, loc. cit.

CHAPTER 7

1. The term was apparently first used by Joseph Priestly (1733–1804). See E. M. Wilbur, *A History of Unitarianism in Transylvania, England and America*, 1952, p. 297.

2. *The Inquirer*, 19 May 1860, p. 413.

3. Reported in *The Inquirer*, 1886, p. 82. E. Lyulph Stanley (1839–1925) later became the 4th Baron Sheffield.

4. Writing of Unitarian liturgies, W. D. Maxwell in *The Book of Common Prayer and the Worship of the Non-Anglican Churches*, 1950, p. 20, says: "Obsessed . . . by their desire to accommodate worship 'to the needs of the modern mind', they all over-emphasised the rational side of worship at the expence of the emotional." The same tendency can, of course, be seen in the work of Dr. Samuel Clarke among the Latitudinarians, and the long history of Latitudinarian and Broad Church dislike of the Athanasian Creed. A. P. Stanley, writing in 1870, said that "the recitation of the Creed had in many English churches become obsolete till it was revived some thirty years ago". See R. E. Prothero and G. G. Bradley, *Life and Correspondence of A. P. Stanley*, II, 1893, p. 233.

5. *The Inquirer*, 1860, p. 413.

6. There were, of course, considerable numbers of working-class Unitarians, especially in the industrial areas, but the congregations were dominated by powerful middle-class families; and in such places as Leicester Great Meeting, for example, while the wealthy middle-class element went to the "church", the working-class element went to the "Sunday school". In some places, such as Halifax, the wealthy sat in one part of the church and the poor in another. Observe R. V. Holt's remark, in *The Unitarian Contribution to Social Progress*, 1938, p. 331, regarding the chapels which were the subject of the Dissenters' Chapels Act of 1844: "These congregations were still mainly composed of members of the middle class engaged in commerce and industry, and their retainers, together with a sprinkling of county families and occasionally a member of the aristocracy."

7. *The Christian Reformer*, V, 1849, p. 685, in a notice regarding the opening of Hope St. Church, Liverpool. All the remaining nineteenth-century Unitarian churches built in Liverpool were likewise designated "churches". That a snobbish motive was a factor behind this Nonconformist Gothic building may be seen from reference to M. S. Briggs, *Puritan Architecture and its Future*, 1946, pp. 38–9, and H. Davies, *Worship and Theology in England*, IV, 1962, pp. 47–8.

8. It is not desired by this remark to suggest that other parties within the Anglican fold or other denominations were without these qualities! But less than justice is often done to the Broad Churchmen and Unitarians in this respect, and the latter, in particular, having regard to their numerical strength, took a disproportionate share in schemes, etc., for social amelioration, as reference to R. V. Holt, *The Unitarian Contribution to Social Progress*, 1938, will show. And the Unitarians and Broad Churchmen do appear to have exhibited a particular blend of these qualities.

9. H. R. Haweis in *The Dead Pulpit*, 1896, p. 3, in reference to the tendency of Broad Church teaching.

10. In *Whitaker's Almanack*, 1859, on p. 158, the number of the total clergy in England is given as 18,000; and on p. 160 the total of Unitarian ministers is given as 289.

Bibliography

The following catalogue, which, of course, is not a complete record of all the works consulted in the preparation of this book, lists all the sources quoted in the notes to establish points made in the text. It does not include titles to which only incidental reference is made in the notes, nor does it repeat the long lists of liturgies given in the notes to Chapter 4. In some sections attention is drawn to the most important books.

Except where otherwise stated, all books were published in London.

1. *Reference Works*

    Crockford's Clerical Directory, 1869, 1962.

    The Dictionary of National Biography, 1885–99; 1st supplement, 1901; 2nd supplement, 1912; (1912–21), 1927.

    The Oxford Dictionary of the Christian Church, ed. F. L. Cross, 1957.

    The New Schaff-Herzog Encyclopaedia of Religious Knowledge, ed. S. M. Jackson, XII, New York and London, 1912.

    Whitaker's Almanack, 1859.

2. *Unitarian Periodicals*

    The Annual Review and History of Literature (1808), VII, printed 1809.

    The Christian Life, 1891.

    The Christian Reformer, 1834, 1836, 1851, 1860, 1863. It should be noted that this periodical, which ran from 1815 to 1863, is, in spite of the name, a different work from the one that follows. The latter ran from 1886 to 1887.

    The Christian Reformer, I and II, 1886; III, 1887.

    The Inquirer, 1856, 1860, 1864, 1886.

    The Monthly Repository, XIII, 1818.

    Occasional Papers, II, 1716. (This was, of course, strictly speaking, an English Presbyterian periodical.)

The Prospective Review, 1850, 1854.

The Theological Review, 1867.

Transactions of the Unitarian Historical Society, V, 1931–4; VII, 1939–42.

The Unitarian Herald, 1863.

3. *Other Periodicals both Religious and Secular*

    The British Weekly, 1887.

    Congregational Quarterly, VIII, 1930.

    Contemporary Review, 1871.

    Dublin University Magazine, 1878.

    Edinburgh Review, 1853.

    Expositor, 1903.

    Good Words, 1878.

    The Listener, 1955.

    Macmillan's Magazine, Cambridge, London, printed 1869.

    The Methodist, 1880.

    The Spectator, 1867.

4. *Other Sources*

    The Free Christian Union Papers. In Dr. Williams's Library, 14 Gordon Square, London, W.C.1.

    Martineau, J., *Letters to W. Knight.* A collection of letters by Martineau to Knight at Manchester College, Oxford.

5. *General Histories*

    Clarke, C. P. S., *Short History of the Christian Church,* 3rd ed., 3rd Impression, London, New York, Toronto, 1956.

    Hallam, H., *Introduction to the Literature of Europe,* I, 4th ed., 1854.

    Perry, G. G., *History of the English Church,* 3 vols., 1887.

    Selbie, W. B., *Non-Conformity,* no date given.

    Skeats, H. S., and Miall, C. S., *History of the Free Churches of England 1688–1891,* 1891.

    Tayler, J. J., *A Retrospect of the Religious Life of England,* 1st ed., 1845.

    A Retrospect of the Religious Life of England, 2nd ed., 1876. This edition contains a survey of "recent developments" by J. Martineau.

    Wand, J. W. C., *A History of the Modern Church,* 1955.

6. *The Eighteenth Century*

   (a) *General Works dealing with Church History*

    Abbey, C. J., and Overton, J. H., *The English Church in the Eighteenth Century,* 1st ed., 2 vols., 1878.

    The English Church in the Eighteenth Century, 2nd ed. (abridged), 1887.

Overton, J. H., and Relton, F., *The English Church 1714–1800*, 1906.

(*b*) *Works dealing with more specific aspects of Religious History and Thought*

Coomer, Duncan, *English Dissent under the Early Hanoverians*, 1946.

Griffiths, O. M., *Religion and Learning—a Study in English Presbyterian Thought from the Bartholomew Ejections (1662) to the Foundation of the Unitarian Movement*, Cambridge, 1935.

Stephen, Leslie, *History of English Thought in the Eighteenth Century*, I, 1st ed., 1876.

Stromberg, R. N., *Religious Liberalism in 18th Century England*, Oxford, 1954.

Tulloch, J., *Rational Theology and Christian Philosophy in England in the 17th Century*, 2nd ed., 2 vols., Edinburgh and London, 1874.

7. *The Nineteenth Century*

(*a*) *General works dealing with Church History*

Carpenter, S. C., *Church and People 1789–1889*, 1937.

Cornish, F. W., *History of the English Church in the Nineteenth Century*, 2 vols., 1910.

Hore, A. H., *The Church in England from William III to Victoria*, II, Oxford and London, 1886.

(*b*) *General works dealing with Religious Thought*

d'Alviella, Count Goblet, *The Contemporary Evolution of Religious Thought*, translated by J. Moden, London and Edinburgh, 1885.

Davies, H., *Worship and Theology in England*, IV, 1962.

Elliott-Binns, L. E., *Religion in the Victorian Era*, 1936.

English Thought: 1860–1900, London, New York, Toronto, 1956.

Hunt, J., *Religious Thought in the Nineteenth Century*, 1896.

Macpherson, Hector, *A Century of Intellectual Development*, Edinburgh and London, 1907.

Moore, E. C., *The History of Christian Thought since Kant*, 2nd Impression, 1947.

Pfleiderer, O., *The Development of Theology in Germany since Kant, and its Progress in Great Britain since 1825*, 1890.

Storr, V. F., *The Development of English Theology: 1800–1860*, 1913.

Wedgwood, J., *Nineteenth Century Teachers*, 1909.

(*c*) *Works dealing with more specific aspects of Religious History and Thought*

Carpenter, J. E., *The Bible in the Nineteenth Century*, London, New York, Bombay, 1903.

Cheyne, T. K., *Founders of Old Testament Criticism*, 1893.

Church, R. W., *The Oxford Movement*, 1891.

Glover, Willis B., *Evangelical Nonconformists and Higher Criticism in the Nineteenth Century*, 1954.

Mineka, F. E., *The Dissidence of Dissent*, Chapel Hill, 1944.

Mozley, T., *Reminiscences Chiefly of Oriel College and the Oxford Movement*, II, 1882.

Ramsey, A. M., *F. D. Maurice and the Conflicts of Modern Theology*, Cambridge, 1951.

Saunders, C. R., *Coleridge and the Broad Church Movement*, Durham, N.C., 1942.

Tuckwell, W., *Pre-Tractarian Oxford*, 1909.

Vidler, A. R., *Theology of F. D. Maurice*, 1948.

Wood, H. G., *Frederick Denison Maurice*, Cambridge, 1950.

8. *Unitarian Histories*

Colligan, J. H., *The Arian Movement in England*, Manchester, 1913.

Davies, V. D., *A History of Manchester College*, 1932.

Evans, G. E., *Antiquarian Notes*, III, 1904.

Vestiges of Protestant Dissent. Largely concerned with the dates of individual chapels and their ministers. Liverpool, 1897.

Gordon, Alexander, *Heads of English Unitarian History*, 1895.

Holt, R. V., *The Unitarian Contribution to Social Progress in England*, 1938.

Lindsey, Theophilus, *Historical View of the State of Unitarian Doctrine and Worship from the Reformation to our own Times*, 1783.

McLachlan, H., *The Unitarian Movement in the Religious Life of England*, 1934. A valuable source of information regarding Unitarian periodical literature, etc., but rather lacking in documentation.

Wilbur, E. M., *A History of Unitarianism—In Transylvania, England, and America*, Cambridge, Mass., 1952. The best general history of Unitarianism.

Our Unitarian Heritage, Boston, 1925.

9. *Unitarian Auto-biographical and Biographical Works*
The chief works in this list are marked with an asterisk.

Armstrong, R. A., *H. W. Crosskey, His Life and Work*, Birmingham, 1895.

Belsham, Thomas, *Memoirs of the Late Reverend Theophilus Lindsey*, 2nd ed., 1820.

Carpenter, J. E., *Life and Work of Mary Carpenter*, ed. 1881.

*James Martineau, 1905. Contains much valuable information about nineteenth-century Unitarianism, but unfortunately lacks an index.

The Centenary Commemoration of the Birth of Dr. William Ellery Channing, no author, published by the British and Foreign Unitarian Association, 1880.

Chadwick, J. W., *William Ellery Channing*, London and Cambridge, Mass., 1903.

Cobbe, F. P., *Life of Frances Power Cobbe, by herself*, 1894.

Craufurd, A. H., *Recollections of James Martineau*, Edinburgh, 1903.

**Drummond, J., and Upton, C. B., *Life and Letters of James Martineau*, 2 vols., 1902.

Gordon, A., *Addresses Biographical and Historical*, 1922.

Herford, Brooke, "Channing and His Works" in *Religion and Modern Thought*, 1893.

Jacks, L. P., *The Confession of an Octogenarian*, 1942.

Memorable Unitarians, no editor, published by the British and Foreign Unitarian Association, 1906.

Robinson, H. C., *Diary, Reminiscences, and Correspondence of Henry Crabb Robinson*, selected and ed. Thomas Sadler, III, 1869.

Solly, H., *These Eighty Years*, I and II, 1893.

Thom, J. H., *Life of the Rev. Joseph Blanco White*, 3 vols., 1845.

Turner, W., *Lives of Eminent Unitarians*, 1840.

Williams, J., *Memoirs of the late Rev. Thomas Belsham*, 1833.

10. *Broad Church Auto-biographical and Biographical Works*

Since no history of the Broad Church exists, the movement is best studied by means of the biographies of its leaders. The most helpful works in this connection are marked with an asterisk.

**Abbott, E., and Campbell, L., *Life and Letters of Benjamin Jowett*, 2 vols., 1897.

Arnold, F., *Robertson of Brighton*, 1886.

Brandl, A., *Life of Coleridge*, English edition by Lady Eastlake, 1887.

**Brooke, Stopford A., *Life and Letters of Frederick W. Robertson*, 2 vols., 1891 ed.

Campbell, J. Dykes, *Samuel Taylor Coleridge*, 2nd ed., 1896.

Campbell, R. J., *Thomas Arnold*, 1927.

Coleridge, S. T., *Biographia Literaria*, ed. J. Shawcross, 2 vols., Oxford, 1907.

Cottle, J., *Reminiscences of Samuel Taylor Coleridge and Robert Southey*, 1847.

Cox, G. W., *Life of J. W. Colenso*, 2 vols., 1888.

*Faber, G., *Jowett: A Portrait with a background*, 1957.

Gillman, J., *The Life of S. T. Coleridge*, I, 1838.

*Jacks, L. P., *Life and Letters of Stopford Brooke*, 2 vols., 1917.

Maurice, F., *The Life of Frederick Denison Maurice*, 4th ed., 2 vols., 1885.

Pearson, H., *Smith of Smiths*, 1934.

*Prothero, R. E., and Bradley, G. G., *Life and Correspondence of A. P. Stanley*, 2 vols., 1893.

Stanley, A. P., *The Life and Correspondence of Thomas Arnold, D.D.*, 2 vols., 8th ed., 1858.

Voysey, C., *An Episode in the History of Religious Liberty in the 19th Century*, Ramsgate, printed Edinburgh, 1871.

Whately, E. J., *Life and Correspondence of Richard Whately*, 1866.

11. *Other Auto-biographical and Biographical Works*

Aubrey, John, *Brief Lives, Chiefly of Contemporaries set down by John Aubrey between the years 1669 and 1696*, ed. A. Clarke, 2 vols., Oxford, 1898.

Baxter, Richard, *Autobiography of Richard Baxter*, ed. J. M. Lloyd Thomas, London and Toronto, 1925.

Bourne, H. R. Fox, *Life of John Locke*, 2 vols., 1876.

Calamy, E., *An Historical Account of My Own Life*, ed. J. T. Rutt, I, 1829.

Nonconformist's Memorial, 2nd ed., III, 1803.

Cross, J. W., *George Eliot's Life*, I, Edinburgh and London, 1885 ed.

Davidson, R. T., and Benham, W., *The Life of Archibald Campbell Tait*, II, London and New York, 1891.

Elson, J. H., *John Hales of Eton*, New York, 1948.

Faber, Geoffrey, *Oxford Apostles*, Harmondsworth, 1954 ed.

Horne, T. H., *Reminiscences Personal and Bibliographical of Thomas Hartwell Horne*, 1862.

Liddon, H. P., *Life of Edward Bouverie Pusey*, I, 1893.

Life of Edward Bouverie Pusey, IV, 1897.

Maizeaux, P. Des, *An Historical and Critical Account of the Life and Writings of William Chillingworth*, 1725.

Meadley, G. W., *Memoirs of William Paley*, 2nd ed., Edinburgh, 1810.

Newman, J. H., *Apologia Pro Vita Sua*, 1864 ed.

Rochefoucauld, Francois de la, *A Frenchman in England, 1784,* ed. Jean Marchand, translated from French by S. C. Roberts, Cambridge, 1933.

Tennyson, H., *Life of Alfred Lord Tennyson,* II, 1897.

Watson, Richard, *Anecdotes of the Life of Richard Watson, Bishop of Llandaff,* 2nd ed., 2 vols., 1818.

Whiston, William, *Memoirs of the Life and Writings of Mr. William Whiston,* 2nd ed., 1753.

Wright, T., *Life of Walter Pater,* I, 1907.

12. *Unitarian Works*

Bache, S., *The True Conditions of Christian Salvation. An Examination of the Sacrificial Efficacy of the death of Christ,* Birmingham, 1854.

Beard, C., *Outlines of Christian Doctrine,* 1859.

Belsham, T., *Christianity Pleading for the Patronage of the Civil Power but Protesting against the aid of Penal Law,* 1820.
The Epistles of Paul the Apostle Translated with an Exposition, I, 1822.
Reflections upon the History of Creation in the Book of Genesis. A Discourse delivered at Warrington, 19 August 1821, 1821.
A Summary View of the Evidence and Practical Importance of the Christian Revelation, 2nd ed., 1809.

Carpenter, Lant, *An Examination of Bishop Magee's Charges Against Unitarians and Unitarianism,* Bristol, 1820.

Clarke, J. F., *Manual of Unitarian Belief,* Boston, U.S.A., 1884.

Cobbe, F. P., *Broken Lights: an Inquiry into the Present Condition and Future Prospects of Religious Faith,* 1864.
Darwinism in Morals and other Essays, 1872

Crosskey, H., *The Unitarians,* Birmingham, 1888.

Evanson, E., *The Dissonance of the Four Generally Received Evangelists,* 2nd ed., Gloucester, 1805.

Greg, W. R., *The Creed of Christendom,* 1851.

Hennell, C. C., *Inquiry concerning the Origin of Christianity,* 1st ed., 1838.

Higginson, E., *The Sacrifice of Christ Scripturally and Rationally Interpreted,* 2nd ed., Hull, 1848.
Spirit of the Bible, 2 vols., 1853–55.

Kenrick, T., *Exposition of the Historical Writings of the New Testament,* 3 vols., Birmingham, 1807.

Kenrick, J., *Unitarianism the Essence of Vital Christianity,* 1817.

Lloyd, W., "Miracles in the Old and New Testaments" in *Religion and Modern Thought,* 1893.

Maginnis, David, *Characteristics of Christian Unitarianism,* London, printed Belfast, 1859.

Martineau, J., *Endeavours after the Christian Life,* 10th ed., 1900.

Essays, Reviews, Addresses, 4 vols., 1890–1.

The Rationale of Religious Inquiry, 1st ed., 1836.

The Rationale of Religious Inquiry, 4th ed., 1853.

The Seat of Authority in Religion, 4th ed., 1898.

Studies of Christianity, 1858.

McLachlan, H., *The Religious Opinions of Milton, Locke, and Newton,* Manchester, 1941.

Newman, F. W., *The Hebrew Monarchy,* 2nd ed., 1853.

Priestley, J., *Notes on all the Books of Scripture, for the use of the Pulpit and Private Families,* I, Northumberland (U.S.), 1803.

Religion and Modern Thought (no editor), published by Philip Green, Essex Street, 1893.

Smith, G. V., *The Prophecies Relating to Nineveh and the Assyrians,* 1857.

Tarrant, W. G., *Our Faith,* 1899.

Tayler, J. J., *An Attempt to Ascertain the Character of the Fourth Gospel,* 1867.

A Catholic Church the Want of Our Time, 1867.

Two Lectures: being the Introduction to a Course on the Early History of Christianity, 1857.

Wellbeloved, C., *Three Letters addressed to the Ven. and Rev. Francis Wrangham, M.A., Archdeacon of Cleveland, in his reply to his Remarks on Unitarianism and Unitarians,* 2nd ed., York, 1823.

White, J. B., *Observations on Heresy and Orthodoxy,* 1835.

Wright, John, *Denials and Beliefs of Unitarians,* 1901.

13. *Broad Church and Latitudinarian Works*

Abbott, E. A., *The Kernel and the Husk,* 1886.

Alford, H., *Essays and Addresses—chiefly on Church Subjects,* 1869.

Arnold, Matthew, *Literature and Dogma,* 4th ed., 1874.

Literature and Dogma, 1883 ed.

Arnold T., *The Christian Life, Its Course, Its Hindrances and Its Helps,* 1841.

Essay on the Right Interpretation and Understanding of Scripture, 1831.

Principles of Church Reform, 4th ed., 1833.

Two Sermons on the Interpretation of Prophecy, Oxford, 1839.

Bibliography

Brooke, Stopford A., *Sermons Preached in St. James's Chapel*, First Series, 13th ed., 1883.

Sermons Preached in St. James's Chapel, Second Series, 7th ed., 1891.

God and Christ, 1894.

Chillingworth, W., *The Religion of Protestants a safe way to Salvation*, Oxford, 1638.

The Works of William Chillingworth, 1742.

The Works of William Chillingworth, Oxford, 1838.

Clark, W. G., *True and False Protestantism*, London and Cambridge, 1871.

Colenso, J. W., *Commentary on the Epistle to the Romans*, Natal, 1861.

Natal Sermons, II, 1868.

The Pentateuch and the Book of Joshua Critically Examined, Part I, 1862.

Coleridge, S. T., *Aids to Reflection*, ed. T. Fenby, Liverpool, 1877.

Confessions of an Inquiring Spirit, ed. H. N. Coleridge, 4th ed., 1863.

The Poetical Works of S. T. Coleridge, ed. W. M. Rossetti, undated.

Unpublished Letters from Samuel Taylor Coleridge to the Rev. John Prior Estlin, ed. Henry A. Bright, undated.

Unpublished Letters of Samuel Taylor Coleridge, ed. E. L. Griggs, I, 1932.

Curteis, G. H., *Dissent and its Relation to the Church of England*, 1871.

Davison, J., *The Nature of Prophecy*, 1st ed., 1824.

Essays and Reviews, 5th ed., 1861.

An Examination of Canon Liddon's Bampton Lectures on the Divinity of our Lord and Saviour Jesus Christ, by a clergyman of the Church of England. Published by Trubner and Co., 1871.

Fremantle, W. H., *Natural Christianity*, London and New York, 1911.

Hales, J., *The Works of the Ever-Memorable Mr. John Hales of Eton*, 3 vols., Glasgow, 1765.

Hampden, R. D., *Observations on Religious Dissent*, Oxon, 1834.

The Scholastic Philosophy considered in its relation to Christian Theology, 2nd ed., 1837.

Haweis, H. R., *The Dead Pulpit*, 1896.

Winged Words, 1885.

Hey, John, *Lectures in Divinity 1796–1798*, I, 3rd ed., Cambridge, 1841.

Hoadly, B., *Plain Account of the Nature and End of the Lord's Supper*, 1735.

Jowett, B., *The Epistles of St. Paul to the Thessalonians, Galatians and Romans with Critical Notes and Dissertations*, 2 vols., 2nd ed., 1859.

Sermons on Faith and Doctrine, ed. W. H. Fremantle, 1901.

Law, Edmund, *Considerations on the Theory of Religion*, new ed., 1820.

Reflections on the Life and Character of Christ, Cambridge, 1760 ed.

Locke, J., *Philosophical Works*, I, 1877.

Maurice, F. D., *The Doctrine of Sacrifice*, 1879 ed.

Sermons Preached in Lincoln's Inn Chapel, V, 1891 ed.

Theological Essays, ed. E. F. Carpenter, 1957.

Theological Essays, 3rd ed., London and New York, 1871.

Milman, H. H., *The History of the Jews*, I, 2nd ed., 1830.

Robertson, F. W., *Lectures and Addresses on Literary and Social Topics*, 1858.

Sermons, 1st series, 1883 ed.

Sermons, 4th series, new ed., 1882.

Stanley, A. P., *Addresses and Sermons delivered during a visit to the United States and Canada in 1878*, 1883.

The Epistles of St. Paul to the Corinthians, with Critical Notes and Dissertations, 2 vols., 1855.

Essays chiefly on Church and State, 1870.

Stillingfleet, E., *Irenicum*, 2nd ed., 1662.

Thirlwall, Connop, "Introduction" in Schleiermacher's *A Critical Essay on the Gospel of Luke*, translated by Thirlwall, 1825.

Tillotson, J., *Sermons*, 1728.

Voysey, C., *The Sling and the Stone*, IV, 1869.

Watson, R., *Miscellaneous Tracts on Religious, Political and Agricultural Subjects*, 2 vols., 1815.

Whately, R., *Essays on Some of the Difficulties in the Writings of St. Paul*, 1828.

Williams, R., *Rational Godliness*, 1855.

14. *Liturgies, Works on Liturgies, and Hymn Books*

The following list, it should be noted, does not repeat the lists of liturgies given in the notes 22 and 25 of Chapter 4 of this book.

Common Prayer for Christian Worship, printed 1900.

Davies, H., *Worship and Theology in England*, IV, 1962.

Although it has been listed earlier under section 7 (*b*), it has been thought worthwhile to repeat the title here, since the volume contains a valuable account of nineteenth-century liturgical practice.

Devotional Offices for Protestant Dissenters at Mansfield, Manchester, 1797.

Martineau, J., *Hymns for the Christian Church and Home*, 1840. *Hymns of Praise and Prayer*, 1874.

Maxwell, William D., *The Book of Common Prayer and the Worship of the Non-Anglican Churches*, 1950.

Peaston, A. E., *The Prayer Book Reform Movement in the 18th Century*, Oxford, 1940. The chief work on this subject. "Nineteenth Century Liturgies" in *Transactions of the Unitarian Historical Society*, VII, 1939–42.

Voysey, Charles, *Revised Prayer Book*, 3rd ed., 1892.

15. *Works relating to Architecture*

Briggs, M. S., *Architecture*, 1947. *Puritan Architecture and its Future*, 1946.

The Churches and Chapels of the East Cheshire Christian Union. Place of publication unspecified, but possibly Manchester. Date not given, but early twentieth century.

Clark, Kenneth, *The Gothic Revival*, 1962 ed.

Drummond, A. L., *The Church Architecture of Protestantism*, Edinburgh, 1934.

Jones, R. P., *Nonconformist Church Architecture*, 1914. Although not referred to in the notes, this book is included here because it is a useful brief introduction to the subject, and, rather interestingly, is written by a Unitarian.

Neale, J. M., and Webb, B., *Durandus*, Leeds, 1843.

Short, H. L., "Changing Styles in Nonconformist Architecture" in *The Listener*, 17 March 1955.

Stanley, A. P., "The Religious Aspect of Gothic Architecture" in *Good Words*, 1878.

16. *Other Works*

Bettenson, H., *Documents of the Christian Church*, 1956.

Bouquet, A. C., *Hinduism*, 1948.

Cambridge Essays, 1856.

Davidson, S., *An Introduction to the New Testament*, 2 vols., 1848. *A Treatise on Biblical Criticism*, Edinburgh, 1852.

De Quincey, Thomas, *Works*, II (Recollections of the Lakes and the Lake Poets), Edinburgh, 1862.

Emerson, R. W., *Works*, published by George Routledge and Sons, undated.

Horne, T. H., *An Introduction to the Critical Study and Knowledge of the Holy Scriptures*, 1st ed., 1818.

An Introduction to the Critical Study and Knowledge of the Holy Scriptures, 2nd ed., 1821.

An Introduction to the Critical Study and Knowledge of the Holy Scriptures, II and IV, 9th ed., 1846.

An Introduction to the Critical Study and Knowledge of the Holy Scriptures, ed. S. Davidson, 10th ed., II, 1856.

An Introduction to the Critical Study and Knowledge of the Holy Scriptures, ed. Tregelles, 10th ed., IV, 1856.

Lamb, C., *Letters of Charles Lamb*, 1888.

McLachlan, H., *English Education under the Test Acts*, Manchester, 1931.

Morley, J., *Critical Miscellanies*, III, London, Edinburgh printed, 1886.

Pusey, E. B., *Daniel, the Prophet*, Oxford and London, 1864.

Schmiedel, P. W., "John, the Son of Zebedee" in *Encyclopaedia Biblica*, II, 1901.

Index

(*N.B.*—The Index does not cover the references made to these subjects in the Notes. The items in italics refer to the *main* discussions of these matters in the text: they are not exhaustive.)

Index

Wigmore — Beddoes

a) Church of england. History